# HIKING AND LIFE LESSONS

## Partial Enlightenment from Death Valley

# KEN ROCK

Mericle Publishing

SAN DIEGO, CA

Published by Mericle Publishing
San Diego, CA

Library of Congress Control Number: 2021910455

Design by Cathy Klein

Editing by Mary McLaughlin, Friendly Pen Editing

Death Valley National Park Map, California and Nevada, United States 1997. Source: U.S. National Park Service

Author photo by Voni Rock

Cover photo by KiskaMedia

Back cover photo by Stone Lawson

All photographs are property of the author and were taken with his camera or cell phone. A few were taken by Brad, John, or Johnny (if Ken is in the photo).

ISBN (print): 978-0-9979503-2-8

ISBN (ebook): 978-0-9979503-3-5

# CONTENTS

# PROLOGUE

We are four guys who like to get immersed in nature when we can. Our aspiration for adventure evolved into having an annual trip together to Death Valley National Park (DVNP). Actually, there was a fifth man who was always with us, though we had never met him: Michel Digonnet. Digonnet is the author of the book *Hiking Death Valley: A Guide to its Natural Wonders and Mining Past*, which provided the initial gravity that drew our foursome into this near-cultish activity together.

I realize that most people have no desire to follow in our footsteps, so I won't try to convince anyone to hike DVNP. It's just that in the last seventeen years, this activity has had way more influence on my life than anything else that consumed only 1 percent of my time. These experiences have significantly shaped me and brought a fullness to my life that is real but difficult to articulate. You might find that as I try to describe them, my self-discoveries could strike something in you—or at least be entertaining.

In the few years when our hike was cancelled for reasons common to four middle-aged men with other obligations, I substituted activities to attempt to fill the gap. This chronicle, therefore, has a few non-Death Valley chapters, and they provide a bit of contrast and perspective. In addition, some life events from this period that seriously pummeled or bolstered me are included where they intersected with the DVNP lessons.

When a project lasts a number of years, it always seems to work out that we were younger when we started than when we ended. John, Brad, Johnny, and I began these trips without any debilitating physical or emotional issues—or without admitting to them. We weren't exactly at our physical primes, but in our forties, we hadn't slowed down too much from our peaks. Neither had our confidence been significantly shaken or diminished. Inevitably, time seems to have a way of changing those less compromised conditions.

In my struggle for enlightenment, or at least less opacity, I am always trying to learn lessons about hiking—and about life. At times, the thoughtful reader may think something less than complimentary about some of my reasoning or actions, and many lessons could appear obvious. Nevertheless, for my personal reinforcement and perhaps your entertainment, at the end of each chapter I list things I've learned each year.

Most people have periodic activities with family or friends that provide a way to track and measure relationships, personal evolution, and life. Maybe those events are reunions, Thanksgivings, vacations at a lake, or Grandma's birthdays. This book might inspire you to ponder the stories, lessons, wonder, and magic that transpire during and between those events. Life is rich, and I believe it is helpful and healthy to take stock of the good things.

Our story has beauty, adventure, fun, isolation, and physical tests—probably to a higher degree than is found in more traditional annual reunions. The emotional conflict and stress that come with modern life are not in this story much, because escaping them is one reason we continually return to Death Valley National Park. Getting grounded by the fundamentals of existence and nature by living out of a backpack for a few days pushes a reset button on all that modern...crap. At least it always does for us.

We do admit, though, that a padded seat, running water, flush toilet, and soft bed with the wife in a controlled climate feel really, really good afterwards. Reliable internal combustion engines seem amazing. It is also true that returning to phones, bills, work demands, and the internet makes us cringe and sigh with resignation every year.

Here are the guides for this series of adventures:

## Bradley Jay: "BJ" or "Brad"

 The youngest by two to five years, Brad is also the most athletic. When he was in his twenties, he was on the World Cup road bicycle racing team. That means that his daily activity involved enduring leg- and lung-busting workouts with the constant threat of breaking bones and losing large portions of skin to asphalt abrasion.

Sure, there was excitement, team comradery, competition, and free travel to new places, and he didn't have to work in an office, but 99 percent of us would not make that trade, even if we had the physical skills to do so.

Brad is still in excellent aerobic condition, and his lanky build and flexibility also make him the best at climbing falls. (A fall is where there would be a waterfall if there were any water, which is a feast-and-[mostly] famine condition in DVNP.) Although highly adventurous and skilled, Brad is fairly considerate and aware of his partners' struggles to keep up and avoid great injury. These DVNP trips are somewhat tamed down from what BJ used to talk his friends into.

Brad is a well-read, thoughtful gentleman. He tends to be the group leader and usually sets the adventure route for the season. It is fortunate for us that he is empathetic to his less physically capable and more risk-averse peers. He usually has the best equipment—stove, sleeping bag, and satellite map thingy.

In real life, Brad manages a retail store and lives in Moorpark, California. He has two boys who have grown to be willing and able to handle their own Dad-led DVNP adventures. His wife is the sister of the next member of the group, Johnny.

## John 1: "Johnny"

In his earlier years, Brad became a friend to Johnny's family. Johnny was raised on a ranch in Moorpark, California before Moorpark became an upscale suburb. His childhood with salt-of-the-earth, yet intellectual parents, his time as a paratrooper in the army, and his martial arts discipline shaped Johnny into a tough individual who seemingly can't be broken by any challenge.

Johnny has worked in a bookstore for most of the last thirty-plus years. He's one of those bookstore clerks who seem to know every author and every book without behaving like a know-it-all. Being a prodigious reader has power-shaped his intellect and added some pounds to his frame. That makes him one of the most interesting—though maybe not the fastest—people to walk with. The martial arts have messed up his knees, but Johnny never seems to have regrets or feel sorry for himself when the hike gets tough.

He brings interesting food on the hikes, such as pate, oysters, and fine cheeses. Not that I ever eat that stuff, but it is interesting. His backpack always wins the "wuss competition" as the lightest, probably because he doesn't carry things like rope, maps, and extra clothes. He often regales us around the campfire (actually a candle or LED light) with quotes from authors or movies that we had forgotten until that moment.

Johnny lives with his wife in Lancaster, California. Lancaster is a fine example of how the Mojave Desert can be transformed when levelled for nice, affordable housing. Working in a bookstore won't make you rich, but it can introduce you to a wealth of fascinating people, some of whom you'll get to work alongside. When Johnny worked at a bookstore in Oxnard, California, one of those fascinating coworkers was John.

## John 2: "John" or "Doogie"

John likes to walk and ride his bike a lot, and he lives in Oxnard, California, where he can do those things comfortably for most of the year. Because of this, he has casually acquired lifelong fitness. John went to the University of California, Santa Barbara (UCSB) and earned a degree in geology. He has a fine memory and is a good scientist, but books are his avocation and first love, allowing for a much broader interest in the world than just studying rocks might yield.

John quickly impresses with how polite, kind, thoughtful, and intelligent he is. One will eventually learn, however, that he is also culturally indifferent in the most imaginative of ways. For example, after work one night, John found a jar of teeth in the parking lot. He decided to keep the teeth, which is weird enough, but then he passed them out in the bookstore on Halloween, dressed in a tutu, carrying a wand, and identifying himself as the Tooth Fairy.

I've never heard John complain in the face of a long and grueling day, expectations gone awry, injury, cold, or other disappointment—including some of the marginal stuff I've given him to eat. He can't keep up with BJ on an uphill grind, and with some of the falls we recently climbed he has required assistance to ascend. He's only human.

John's pack is usually heavy, burdened with books and extra stuff that is sometimes so nice to have. A better adventure companion one could not find. That companionship and fun intellect were reasons why he was my best friend at UCSB, where we were both geology students.

It's too tempting to tell a couple more stories about Doogie. We were in a physics class for science and engineering majors, taught in a large lecture hall. There was dead silence when the final exam was passed out and a hundred students opened the pages to face their fates. A few seconds later John burst out, "OH NO!" The raucous laughter that followed was a marvelous break to the tension in the room. He survived the exam, though. A few years later, at the formal and so-serious college graduation ceremony, after getting his diploma on stage, Doogie faced the audience and tore open his gown—revealing a Superman logo.

## Ken: Usually just "Ken"

This guy is me. I am one of the weaker siblings in a family of superior athletes. I love the outdoors, which drew me into studying environmental studies and geology, and those subjects served as reasons to hike more. I was an avid distance bicyclist and raced some. My modest successes were outweighed by the required time and personal costs—and the fact that I hate crashing. For those reasons, I ultimately recognized that it would be unwise to pursue bike racing as a lifestyle.

I ended up in the water and wastewater business, where my restless, progressive, and rebellious management style caused me to move to a few jobs in California, Nevada, and finally Arizona, where I now reside with my mostly tolerant wife, Voni. Perhaps it is not coincidental that nowhere I've lived has been further than a day's drive from DVNP.

Although I was a good student, I don't read too much. I enjoy my leisure, but I'm perpetually unsettled. Music inspires me to joy or tears, but I am only a fair guitarist and singer, if you are generous with compliments. I love nature but greatly appreciate home life. I am a dedicated environmentalist with a road motorcycle. I have a sketchy memory, but I'm mechanically adept and resourceful. I am the oldest in this clan by a few years yet no wiser for it. I can be useful for interpreting topographic maps and moving heavy objects.

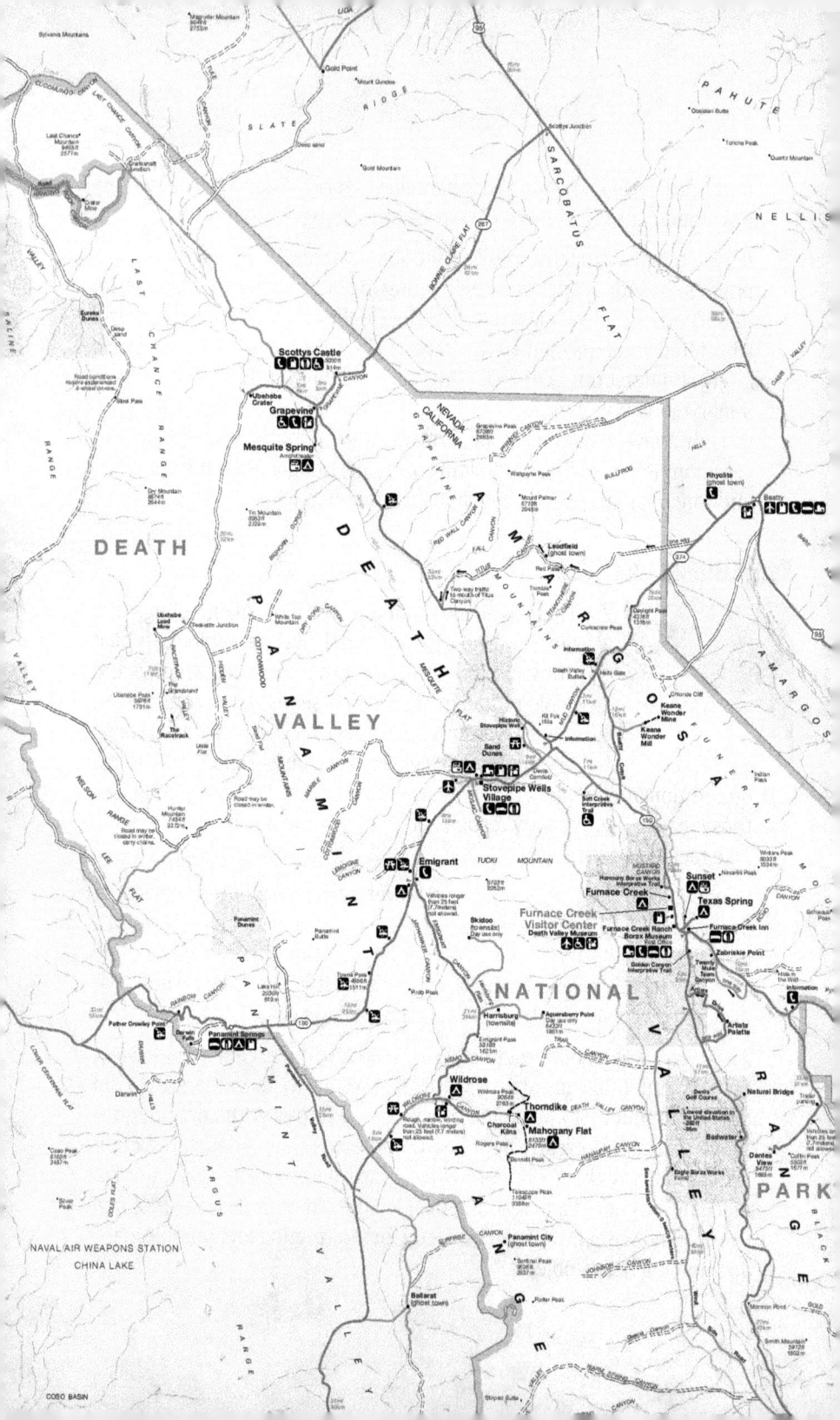

DEATH

VALLEY

NATIONAL

PARK

PANAMINT RANGE

AMARGOSA RANGE

FUNERAL MOUNTAINS

GRAPEVINE MOUNTAINS

DEATH VALLEY

LAST CHANCE RANGE

PANAMINT VALLEY

NEVADA
CALIFORNIA

PAHUTE

NELLIS

NAVAL AIR WEAPONS STATION
CHINA LAKE

COSO BASIN

Sylvania Mountains
Slate Ridge
Gold Point
Mount Gundee
Scottys Junction
Obsidian Butte
Tonopah Peak
Quartz Mountain
Gold Mountain

Scottys Castle
Ubehebe Crater
Grapevine
Mesquite Spring

Rhyolite (ghost town)
Beatty

Leadfield (ghost town)

Eureka Dunes
Last Chance Mountain

Ubehebe Lead Mine
The Racetrack

Stovepipe Wells Village
Sand Dunes
Historic Stovepipe Well

Emigrant
Skidoo (townsite)

Furnace Creek Visitor Center
Death Valley Museum
Furnace Creek
Furnace Creek Ranch
Borax Museum
Furnace Creek Inn
Sunset
Texas Spring
Zabriskie Point

Panamint Springs
Father Crowley Point
Darwin Falls
Darwin

Wildrose
Charcoal Kilns
Thorndike
Mahogany Flat

Harrisburg (townsite)
Aguereberry Point

Artists Palette
Natural Bridge
Devils Golf Course
Badwater
Dantes View
Eagle Borax Works

Panamint City (ghost town)
Ballarat (ghost town)

Golden Canyon Interpretive Trail
Twenty Mule Team Canyon
Hole in the Wall

# WHY DEATH VALLEY?

It seems best to start by answering the question that people frequently ask us: "What did you do on vacation while the wife was at home?" First of all, the answer is that with the way that we approach DVNP, our wives have no interest whatsoever in accompanying us. They may, someday, share parts of this national park with us by staying in a park motel and eating in restaurants. (This response also helps to establish that these women are normal, as measured by the vast majority of our society. They only married men who tinker with the fringe of normal.) I think our wives' attitudes towards us is one more of tolerance than amusement. I should probably ask them that question if the timing ever feels right and I'm medicated well enough to accept the response.

The second answer is that DVNP is close enough for us to drive to in a day, and it offers challenges that we four guys apparently feel a need to test ourselves with. Lots of people do things like skydive, ride a motorcycle, jet ski, snowboard, mountain bike, skateboard, rock climb, etc., for no better reason than to feel the thrill of accomplishment. I think that in modern life we invent ways to test ourselves because, for many of us, daily existence is too tame and boring unless we enhance it with some excitement. I also believe that our trips often become more challenging than they really needed to be, but that does make for more interesting stories. We have always come back home from them, anyway. At least, we have so far.

John has a tee shirt that says "Hike Death Valley" with an illustration of a happy skeleton with a hiking hat and boots walking across a vast, bleak landscape. That is a fair assessment of what would happen to a person attempting to hike the valley floor in summer. I know this from a similar experience I had when dating my wife in the summer, when she lived in Phoenix, Arizona, and I lived in coastal California. It was over 110 degrees Fahrenheit and I "needed" a run, so decided to trot six or so miles into the nearby Phoenix Mountain Preserve. I'd never required water on so short a run before, so insisted to her that I needn't be burdened by it. I returned an hour later looking like that skeleton, without the smile. OK, that lesson was learned.

The valley floor of DVNP in the summer is usually only several degrees hotter than Phoenix or Las Vegas. The biggest difference is that there is virtually no shade and only a few places over long distances where water and air conditioning offer refuge. No fun. Dangerous. Even we four are not that stupid and desperate for adventure.

But there are seasons—even in DVNP. And contrary to the name, this national park consists of much more than a big, dry, dead valley below sea level. So, we explore higher places and canyons that the hiker-prophet Digonnet describes in his book, and we go in winter. Sometimes we find spring water to filter and drink. Occasionally we find abandoned mines and buildings if shelter is desired, but the weather is usually temperate enough that we don't need something overhead. The structures are often dilapidated and unsafe anyway.

Here is some background about Death Valley, with a lot of help from Digonnet, to help you appreciate the place:

Due to its isolation, infamous heat, and foreboding name, even with the 1849 California Gold Rush pulling settlers and miners westward, virtually all of the white men entering Death Valley at that time just tried to survive crossing it. They did not typically encounter the sparse number of Native Americans who lived in a few canyons near springs. In the 1860s, a little mining began in Death Valley, and this exploration and mining was accelerated by the 1872 Mining Law. This law's brazen intention was to encourage the exploration and settling of the west, our nation's proclaimed manifest destiny. All one had to do to begin digging up the landscape on federal land was to register a claim that a valuable mineral might be available. (The 1872 Mining Law, by the way, is still in effect but fortunately conditioned by more recent environmental constraints.)

The popularized twenty-mule-team borax mine was established in the 1880s, and in the first decades of the 1900s most of the many other mines were started. In some places, a few thousand miners and their hardy but equally deluded supporters rushed in to try and make their fortunes, but by the 1930s most of the mines had been abandoned. Harsh conditions, bad roads, and long hauls to any civilization made only the richest ores profitable, and those highly concentrated deposits were more imagined than there in fact. There were improved roads and access by the 1930s and a few new explorations happened, but by then, the area's 1933 national monument status restricted development to existing claims. Death Valley was greatly enlarged and finally granted national park status in 1994.

Current visitors to DVNP who are somewhat intrepid can explore the abandoned endeavors of these miners, who had no legal or moral compulsion to clean up or restore the sites that they tore into. Alas, the vastness of the area means that even dozens of small mines don't significantly alter the landscape. The infrequent but massively strong flash floods in Death Valley will eventually carry away or bury the remaining mining evidence.

The abandoned burros and escaped horses of the original miners have ancestors that still range higher parts of DVNP and may perhaps continue to do so after nature has completely erased all of the mines. Ironically, these hardy and magnificent quadrupeds are probably the most destructive human-introduced aspects of this national park. They have no natural predators, and they consume the sparse brush in the moderate elevations that so desperately hangs on in the meager rainfall there. I love seeing these animals, but they shouldn't be there.

At 5,264 square miles, DVNP is the largest national park in the lower forty-eight states. It is larger than the states of Rhode Island, Delaware, and Connecticut. DVNP has four major mountain ranges, which are divided into some smaller ranges. It's so big that when you enter the park, it could still take several hours of driving to arrive at your destination within it. With all of these mountains and what they contain, we could explore something new every year until we are unable to drive or walk. I hope that will be true for us.

Despite being so large, DVNP is not between any population clusters of more than a few thousand people. It is surrounded by an even greater area of mostly unspoiled desert. For certain, most people do not get here by accident. The park is all in eastern California, except for a small triangle in Nevada. Geologically speaking, Death Valley is a continuation of the desolate basin and range desert of northern Nevada.

My geology training is decades old and insufficient to do justice to this place, and I've been informed that the vocabulary sounds like pretentious gibberish to many people. I will say that the mountains contain formations more than hundreds of millions of years old and that the basin floor has been periodically flooded, often with large lakes, most recently about 2,000 years ago—hence the large playas (former beaches, now low flat areas) of dried mud and salts. I'll make a few geological references in some chapters, but they'll be in simple terms that everyone can understand, because that's all I can remember.

The current average of less than two inches of annual rainfall in Death Valley means that the rocks are not dressed in vegetation. For most years and most everywhere below about 7,000' elevation, anything that grows in DVNP, except where the rare springs are, is just sparse decoration. It is barren, rough, and magnificent earth everywhere.

Since vegetation is essential for fauna, our encounters with any animals are rare, so I'll mention them with each year's account. A remarkable exception was during my first and solo DVNP visit in the spring of 1994. It was during spring break, and the park was relatively busy. The large number of park visitors had come that year because of a rare and significant rain a few weeks before, and the opportunistic wildflowers were magnificent. Plants and flowers never truly blanket the open lower desert there, but the tiny dots of color add a dazzling sparkle. In that year, with those flowers came about a billion caterpillars, and despite my efforts to dodge them with the motorcycle, the road was awash with caterpillar guts. Apparently, the cars were less successful at evading the critters.

A contest in Death Valley with no winner

I had come for just an overnight visit and barely had time to visit Scotty's Castle before finding a place to park the motorcycle off-road and camp, as all of the campgrounds were full. Before the sun set, I climbed to the top of the nearby large hill for a spectacular view, and my cycle was just a dot below. On the way back, I saw something that very few ever see. Circled around a tiny bush were a snake and lizard, locked in a time-frozen death grip on each other's throats. The image stays burned in my memory as a life contest for superiority that resulted in a no-win tragedy. That qualifies as my first DVNP lesson.

**2003**

# Lower Marble Canyon
## *An Auspicious Beginning*

It doesn't take much for John to convince me to tag along on this group trip. My father had regaled me with stories of Death Valley motorcycle rides in the 1970s, when I was too busy being a college student to accompany him. Then there was my short but magical 1994 overnight solo ride there. I have never met his friends, but John is interesting company and I can keep up with him physically, so this trip seems a fine idea. Fortunately (actually not so), I still have my thirty-year-old hiking gear.

However, John does have to convince me that this adventure won't be quite as fate challenging as some of the previous trips that he's taken with BJ and Johnny. There was their assault on Mount Whitney one winter, where they returned to their 12,000' elevation base camp to find that half of their gear had been blown away, far down the mountain; four men spent that night in one two-man tent with two sleeping bags. Another winter adventure of theirs was climbing 11,049-foot Telescope Peak in DVNP, resulting in a fall causing deep gashes in John's legs from ice crampons. For this lower Marble Canyon trip, their fourth team member has dropped out, so there is an opening for me. When invited to this first adventure, I mention that I am prone to hypothermia and that I don't care to invest in whatever it takes to sleep in snow. John assures me there will be no snow camping this year. He even reveals that he is probably cured of ever wanting to camp in the snow again.

John says that traversing lower Marble Canyon is going to be just a hike, and how could anyone get lost in a canyon? John also says that it is not too high or too low in elevation, and there are beautiful, polished canyon walls with some petroglyphs. He makes it sound interesting and not very risky. My wife has no premonitions of something dangerous that's about to happen. I'm in!

John and I are asked to bring our gear to Brad's house at 9:00 p.m. Being the newcomer, I don't want to question things, but I do know that Death Valley is about five hours away. In the small region of my brain that thinks conventionally, daylight is preferred for hiking, sleep is usually helpful each night, and it seems odd that we might be leaving at some time slightly after 9:00 p.m. Well, it is going to work out, just not how I thought it would.

When John and I bring our ready-to-go packs into the house, we find the living room floor spread with most of what might go with Johnny and Brad—but not everything—and some stuff that won't be needed. Thoughtfully, they want to make sure we have the opportunity to review any packing, including our own. My stuff is ready, or so I think at the time, so I mostly watch the group dynamics and try to fit in. It is about 2:00 a.m. when we leave, which is actually perfect timing for getting to the border of DVNP at daybreak.

Adrenaline works its magic tonight, keeping us mostly alert in anticipation of a new adventure. Adding to the energy is a steady stream of music by the Grateful Dead. I didn't know more than a couple of Grateful Dead tunes when we left, but in Brad's minivan I believe we hear much of their repertoire. Yep, I know the Grateful Dead now.

The roads in DVNP are listed collectively in the Reader's Digest book *The Most Scenic Drives in America*. Entering from the west side over the Cottonwood Mountains at sunrise with no other traffic, and being somewhat adrenaline charged, is magical. The vistas of valleys and mountain ranges, clear of air or light pollution, are something that few other places can compare to in majesty. All of the paved roads in DVNP are two lane and in good condition. There are even more miles of unpaved roads, which vary from passable by a regular sedan to challenging even to a four-wheel-drive high-clearance vehicle.

Getting to the Furnace Creek Visitor Center and ranger station at around 8:00 a.m. is pretty cool too. Besides talking with rangers about our plans and getting a permit, we get to have a hearty breakfast and use the modern restroom, two aspects that we would not experience for a few days after that. Actually, seeing or talking with anyone else wouldn't happen during that period either.

We pile back into the minivan, and Brad steers us back to Stovepipe Wells at the eastern base of the Cottonwood Mountains and then up primitive Cottonwood Canyon Road. After 10.8 miles, the road gets so bad that we park the van and begin the process of putting everything on our backs.

Those moments when you transition from modern transportation to hiking for three days are exciting yet stressful. You know that if you aren't ready, it's too late to wish you had prepared better. You expect some difficulties but believe that the adventure will make it worth the trouble. You hope that the path won't be too difficult and that your choice of partner has been smart. It feels a bit like getting ready to walk down the aisle for marriage, sans the minister, audience, and expectation of lots of sex. In the case of Johnny and BJ, they may have had a nervous feeling similar to committing to an arranged marriage to someone that they were told would be perfect.

When we start out, I have running shoes on and the other three guys wear hiking boots. Brad decides after a half mile that his hiking boots will soon give him blisters, so we wait while he hoofs it back to the car and trades out his boots for running shoes. Back in my twenties when I had field geology classes, the same thing happened to me several times. After loads of blisters, I just parked the hiking boots and transitioned to running shoes for all of my hiking and trail running. It occurs to me that maybe now I should get some better hiking boots, as I'm almost twice as old as I was when I had those experiences. Today, though, the running shoes seem like a good idea for both Brad and me.

Bending with the tilted strata

The next 2.6-mile stretch is a loose gravel road, up the wash to the road's end. Sometimes the gravel is deep, making it unpleasant to walk uphill because the gravel doesn't support our feet evenly and we lose a few inches with every step. The start of our hike also has the shock of a large backpack, which is at its heaviest because we have the most water at this point. Still, the sight of the canyon's narrow opening lifts our spirits. We have made it to the first goal of heading up lower Marble Canyon, at 1,815' elevation. Hey, and it's only about noon.

This hike, like most of those that Digonnet writes about and seemingly every one that we will select to tackle, has no trail. There are good reasons why most people hike on trails! Trails are constructed by experts to minimize environmental impact while grooming a path that is scenic and without undue hardship. It is amazing how much easier it is to walk on a prepared trail than to just follow, or defy, geographic features. In the narrows, the smooth sand is easier to walk on than the gravel road. Once out of the narrows, though, the canyon, where there never was a road (or trail), is more challenging. In these open stretches, the floor consists of braided courses of loose gravel and cobbles from previous stream flows, and there are no straight lines.

On flat ground with a smooth surface and no pack, most people can walk three miles per hour, and athletes like Brad are good for over four miles per hour. With packs, uneven surfaces, and breaks to rest and take pictures, we are averaging about one mile per hour. Sometimes I walk with Brad at his faster pace, but that is exhausting, so usually I hang back with the other two. It doesn't seem like anyone could get lost and, besides, Brad has the maps.

John's interested in the type and composition of the rocks in the walls, some of which he studies with a hand lens. In some places the strata are evenly tilted, while in other spots they are contorted as if plastic. Johnny's comments tend to be along the lines of "Cool!" Brad says things about how awesome the hike is. We all enjoy the strange petroglyphs we find, carved by Native Americans hundreds of years ago. A couple of the images look like flying saucers. No lie—flying saucers.

Today, Marble Canyon is now completely dry, as predicted. The narrows, with nearly vertical walls of polished marble and dolomite (a blue-gray marble, having manganese in it), are astounding. These narrow places are between thirty and seven feet wide, and in one spot Brad demonstrates how he can span the canyon by suspending himself horizontally across the narrow, a couple of feet above the sand. At the upper end of the first narrow, there is a rounded chock stone blocking the canyon. It's as big as a car, giving us some-

thing fun to climb over. We take
some playful pictures there and
on the tilted strata, pretending to
surf down it or bend along with
it. When there is a clear view to
the peaks above the canyon walls,
they are 1,000 feet above us. There
are giant carved scoops in the
marble rock walls and high debris
piles on some opposite sides of
the canyon. This is a wonderfully
scenic hike now.

I was a competent geolo-
gy student at the morphology
(shape) of things, so I've pieced
together with John how this canyon was shaped: flash floods. Almost all of the time, almost every

**Brad spans lower Marble Canyon.**

year, the rains cause a nice little stream of water to flow down the canyon,
moving pebbles and watering plants. We are hiking in those dried-up stream
paths. A flash flood happens when an intense storm is stuck above an area
that drains into a narrow place such as this. The water collects scary-fast
and builds into a wall of mud, rocks, and uprooted trees, rushing down the
canyon, scouring or obliterating everything in its path. A flash flood can move
objects as large as that chock stone, which has to weigh ten tons or more.
The debris flows polish the marble walls and form these carved-out areas.
As it subsides, the flash flood leaves some junk piles on the inside parts of
bends, as we also observe here.

Human survivors of flash floods are rare; they have managed to clamber
up the canyon wall in the scant minute before the roaring cataclysm hits.
Rarer still are the few who were stripped and flailed, lungs filled with mud,
and yet managed to survive the ride in feats of superhuman desperation. I
glance at the cloudless sky and vow to keep this geologic process in mind
with our campsite selection.

There are no other people. The silence is something that we never get
in our regular daily lives. The canyon is so quiet we don't even hear any
Grateful Dead.

Something else is happening too. All of my hiking partners have new,

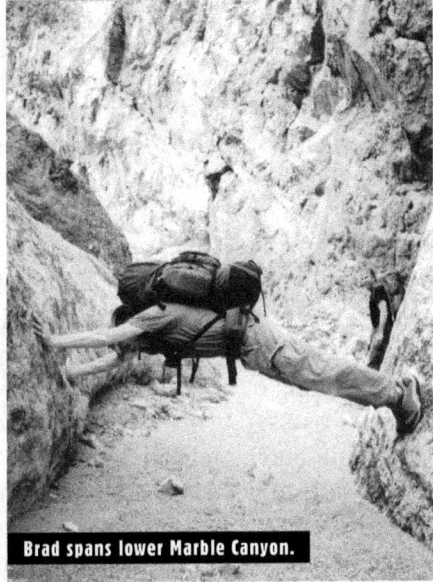

large, soft backpacks. I'm wearing a framed "classic" Kelty pack that was a revolutionary design in 1972 when I bought it but that I haven't worn in, oh, twenty-eight years. The backpack's pads have hardened to something akin to wood. My shoulders and hips are progressing from sore to bruised. I begin to wonder what else in my ancient assemblage of equipment will prove interesting. Ah, yes, there shall be more.

The afternoon hours pass this way: Brad surges ahead, usually alone, and then stops every half hour or so for us to catch up with him and take a brief rest before continuing. There are delightfully shady areas in the several narrows where we stop to admire the polished stone and sit in the cool sand. We keep marching west up the main flow path, passing some side canyons that feed from our right, the north. As it gets toward late afternoon, we come across a spring in the floor of the wash. The flow is maybe one gallon per minute, but it is enough to wash in. Near this spring, one of the canyon walls is a steep slope of packed earth and rock rather than vertical rock. In the narrow wash there are some small pockets of sand, perfect for laying a sleeping bag on. We decide that this is about the best spot that we could hope to find to spend the night, and we're all weary. The slope is not too steep to clamber up, so it will service as our toilet away from the water as well as the potential escape route from a flash flood.

Our dinners are freeze-dried packaged meals; we add a couple of cups of hot water and they cook in the bag. These things are marvelous technological achievements, heavenly after a hard hike. I also discover that butane camp stoves have come a long way since mine was made, and Brad's tiny stove boils water three times faster than my antique. We spread out our bedding close enough to talk but far enough to not hear one another's snores or farts, which almost works.

We didn't bring tents because of the predicted good weather, extra weight, and lack of dangerous creatures (we thought). That allows us to gaze at the Milky Way and meteors, things that are never visible from the homes of almost any Americans. This therapeutic sight alone makes the long walk worthwhile. We have casual conversation about subjects such as the vastness of the universe, the incredibly long stretch of time, and the insignificance of our species. My friends take to reading their books with head lamps, and I just fall asleep, no longer worried about a flash flood.

Nights are long on winter hikes, as you are too tired to stay up much past when it is dark and generally too cold to want to get out of the sack before full light or a full bladder provide enough motivation. The long rest is not begrudged tonight, especially after not sleeping last night.

It takes a little longer in the morning to get rolling on a hike than when you're at home. Granted, your hygiene routine is abbreviated, but you still have to eat and dress. And unlike a regular day, where you just take a few things to the office, everything you own has to be packed away and carried on your back. A pattern begins in which Brad is the first to be ready, as he arises first and he has a "just stuff it" philosophy for packing. "It's called a stuff sack because that's what it is," he says. Johnny is second, I think because of his minimalist collection. Doogie and I take several minutes more to ready our packs.

The plan is to continue up Marble Canyon to the top for the rest of the day and consider from there our hike down. Which direction to walk now is therefore simple: up the canyon. We don't get more than a few hundred feet before we encounter a twenty-five-foot-high half-frozen waterfall, fairly lush with plant growth. Nearby we find a few piles of bighorn sheep bones, including a skull, spinal cord, and jaw. It seems that this watering hole, with boulders and brush, is also a perfect ambush point for a mountain lion, the largest predator in DVNP. Huh, imagine that we should see evidence of the rarest animal in our first visit? So much for not worrying about dangerous beasts.

Climbing the fall is easy work for a spider monkey or BJ, but less so for me, as the pack throws my center of mass back, making me want to fall away. After expressing my challenge, John and Johnny opt for us to haul their packs up with ropes. The footing isn't great, but the guys manage it, and we move forward. John and Brad, who possess Digonnet's book, wonder why he hadn't mentioned this obstacle in his usually thorough narration.

We also reason that the water from this fall had only temporarily disappeared before surfacing as the spring at our campsite. With all the dead sheep parts in the stream, we're glad we brought drinking water and didn't do more than wash a bit in the spring.

Uphill from this point the wash isn't so steep, but at times there is quite a bit of thorny vegetation to push through. Brad and I have long pants, but John and Johnny don't. Their legs end up looking like they've been in a battle with angry cats. The canyon is getting wider and the walls less steep. Hmm, John and Brad say that Digonnet didn't describe upper Marble Canyon like this, but it seems impossible to get lost in a canyon, and we are having a pleasant walk. On this second day we are already hitting our stride, and we keep moving all morning. By about noon we come into a broad, rolling, partially grassy area, a mile open in all directions. I reveal that my altimeter shows us to be at about 5,000' elevation. We scout around and explore a tall mound of large granite boulders. Next to the rocks is the skeleton of a horse. A few hundred yards away we see three wild horses, an exciting sight for all of us that we will never duplicate in all our visits to DVNP. This looks like an idyllic high prairie for a horse to live—and die. We have found a beautiful place for lunch.

Brad checks his map and then his satellite-based locator. They don't seem to match each other or my altimeter. John studies his topographic map and the narration of Digonnet, and they don't describe this location in Marble Canyon either. Ah, well—such a perfect spot to take off the packs and rest! John and Johnny indulge in a little nap in the perfect weather. Brad further explores the high prairie. I sit and try to pretend I'm still a semi-competent field geology student, studying the topographic maps compared to the landscape, compass, and altimeter.

In a bit, we reconvene. Using my best management-by-discussion-and-agreement tactics, I explain that as far as I can tell, this surrounding topography is not on these maps. Because of that, we don't really know where we are or how to get to Marble Canyon. Marble Canyon must have been one of those side contributory canyons that we noted on the way up. A little discussion proceeds, with a tinge of anxiety. We reason that what we do know is how to get back to a good campsite and how to return from there to the car. There is a bit more discussion but not any dissent.

Well, this isn't bad, really. We don't know the name of where we are, but that does not significantly detract from it. Things look different from the opposite direction, so our scenery will seem fresh as we walk back. There won't be any surprises in our path. Downhill is always easier than uphill. We're all feeling good, healthy, and safe. We have avoided the potential disaster of walking blindly into nobody-knows-where, and now we have a nice adventure to and from an unknown place. Hiking with such positive people makes all the difference between angst and anger or enjoyment of the marvels of the day. There is no grief and little regret in our turning around.

Back down the wash we go, through the brush, down the icy fall, and to our familiar campsite, where we arrive as the sun sets. We know the routine here. What has given us something to consider, though, is that we are now running low on water. Upper Marble Canyon has springs, but it turns out that we kind of missed upper Marble Canyon. We are not going to drink the water downstream from an animal drinking-and-dying station without some form of purification. No problem—Brad has a water filtration pump! Oops, new problem—the pump is broken. Now we're on water rations. At least we have enough to cook dinner.

Still, all in all, this is another nice evening with perfect weather and a wonderful night sky. The difference tonight, after seeing the bones from cougar kills, is that we sleep with our knives handy.

The next morning, I rummage in the Kelty backpack and find my three-decade-old iodine disinfection tablets. We fill empty bottles from the meager spring and put a tab in each. My business is water and wastewater treatment, but what happens next is outside my training—the clear water quickly becomes cloudy and pink, with a precipitate falling to the bottom of each bottle. There is no declaration on the ancient label of any coagulant that is part of these tablets, nor an advisory to expect this reaction. Wow, yikes. We reason that high-iodine water is better than no water, so I decant the pink water and discard the precipitate. It doesn't taste completely horrible, but we are definitely going to drink the remainder of our original water stores first. These guys are real troopers, and they act grateful that we have a gallon of weird pink water on hand. Back at the car we have lots of water and electrolyte to drink, so providing that we don't encounter a barrier to getting back today, we'll be OK.

Downhill, even in a sand wash, is much faster and easier than uphill. The packs have less food and water weight, and we are motivated not to drink pink iodine water. I also have the additional speed incentive of bruised shoulders from the wooden backpack pads, so most of my walking is done with my hands up high on the straps, trying to pull the weight off my shoulders and hips. We enjoy the mountains around us and the narrows, but we don't take nearly as many breaks. I'm sure the others are getting as parched as me, but there are no complaints. We find by about noon that the minivan is waiting for us. It may sound weird, but it is always a relief to discover that, somehow, our vehicle is still exactly where we left it. We all dump our packs and enjoy fresh water and no weight on our backs.

Returning to the start of what we call conventional life, even after only three days, is weird. We know what to do and how to do it, but it all seems a bit too easy and comfortable. At the same time, knowing that you have to drive for five hours and then unpack and clean everything is a bit sad and sobering. There are bills and work awaiting us. At least the memories and photos will last, along with the sense of accomplishment and comradery.

Once home, Brad checks the maps in his copy of *Hiking Death Valley*. It turns out that we had hiked up the appropriately named Deadhorse Canyon.

About half a mile before the spring where we camped, we had walked past the last apparent side canyon to the north, which was upper Marble Canyon. The four of us mistakenly thought we were taking the main canyon.

As promised (threatened?) here are some lists of things learned:

## Hiking Lessons

1. *Test everything days before you leave, so that things can be replaced in time.*

2. *Old equipment means that it may not be OK anymore. See #1 above.*

3. *When you are going upstream, it is sometimes hard to tell what the main artery/canyon is and what the side/contributory ones are. In contrast, while going downstream, it is almost always fail-safe to eventually find the main canyon. That's just the way water flow works.*

4. *Scrupulously checking your location on detailed maps along the way might keep you on your intended path—if that matters. Alternatively, maybe later you can figure out where you were.*

5. *Hiking with good and capable people, besides keeping you from being lonely, is fun and interesting.*

## Life Lessons

1. *Just because you didn't end up where you thought you would doesn't mean that the trip was bad or the destination not worthwhile. Enjoy it. Maybe it's even better than what you had planned.*

2. *We're smarter and more successful when we work together.*

3. *Dare to do things you haven't done in places you haven't been. Memories get made that way. That is important stuff for an enjoyable life.*

4. *Choose friends wisely when taking an adventure. Alternatively, get real lucky.*

5. *Sometimes adrenaline can replace most of the need for sleep.*

6. *Why would there be petroglyphs hundreds of years old of flying saucers unless...?*

Doogie wishes that he'd seen the flying saucers too.

# 2004

# Upper Marble Canyon & Deadhorse Canyon

*Johnny Quest*

I have a minivan, a Nissan Quest, which was highly useful when raising three daughters. The girls are grown now, but the car also has enough room for four guys and their large backpacks. I offer to use our minivan on our next trip, feeling obliged to make some contribution to these ventures. What I don't have is a copy of *Hiking Death Valley*, so I can't make trip suggestions. Neither can I evaluate any ideas that are given. Maybe it is just as well, because if I'd had more narrative about where we were going, I might not have been so eager to take the minivan.

Ah, but for now I am young(ish), confident, and bold, albeit a bit naive. John has come over to my house so that he and my wife, Voni, can laminate maps of the Marble Canyon area, hoping to keep us from getting lost this time. The plastic lamination protects the maps from sweat and rain. John and Voni are up until about 2:00 a.m. for our sakes. I've also invested in a water filter, so what more preparation could I need?

We are once again going to the western flank of the Cottonwood Mountains, at the north end of the Panamint Range. Brad's idea is to try last year's Marble Canyon hike from the top, hike down to where we made our wrong turn, purposely go up Deadhorse Canyon and find our way back to the car. We now have more detailed maps, and much of the scenery will be new from the top of the canyon. The dirt road we are taking, I find later, is rated as usually requiring four-wheel-drive vehicles with high clearance. For those who don't know, a Quest minivan is neither four-wheel drive nor high clearance.

Rather than listen to all of the Grateful Dead again, I have brought along my collection of Loudon Wainwright III recordings. I love Loudon Wainwright, but I can now say with some certainty that several early morning hours spent listening exclusively to Loudon is not better than the same amount of time spent listening to the Grateful Dead. I know three other men who would agree. I switch artists before the irritation becomes too great.

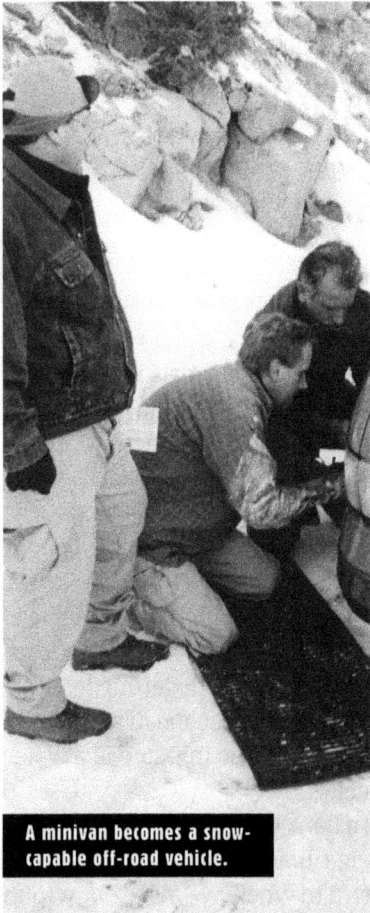

A minivan becomes a snow-capable off-road vehicle.

It is a cold January, and we get to our turn-off in early morning. Before getting to the western park boundary, we turn off Highway 190 onto the dirt Saline Valley Road. The road starts out smooth and easy to navigate. It recently rained, or more accurately as we climb in elevation, snowed, so driving traction worsens. One thing I did do properly was pack cables for the tires, just in case. That just-in-case point happens about ten miles along this dirt road, in a combination of snow and mud. I get out to install the cables, and the cold sends me into convulsive shivers, making me useless. Apparently, my premonition about being sensitive to hypothermia is accurate. Johnny gives me his down vest and orders me back into the minivan. My friends effectively install the cables on the front tires so that their thawing driver can proceed.

The dirt road is narrow with no guard rails, and we are somewhere we've never been, in a minivan that is surely not intended for this application.

We continue to proceed successfully, not because I'm some amazingly skilled driver but more likely because I'm fearfully cautious. Five miles later, near South Pass at 5,997' elevation we meet a Jeep SUV coming from the other direction and slow so that we can share the narrow road. This is the only vehicle we will see in DVNP for the whole trip. The driver looks at us as if we are complete idiots, and I gamely smile back at her.

We now must descend a slightly muddy and snowy primitive dirt road, but we are emboldened by our unlikely success to this point. By going very slowly and steering around anything that could further impair traction, we make it to the bottom of the road without much drama. It is dry and considerably warmer here. I am nervous that the weather might worsen, meaning that our chances of climbing out of here on the only available road will decrease to zero. I haven't figured out what to do if that happens, since there is no phone coverage and nobody around to help us. If the Quest does not start, we are just as stuck. At this moment I feel like this has been a little underplanned, but there isn't much to do but hope for clear weather and try to enjoy the coming hiking adventure. There seems to be no point in spreading worry to my partners, who at least outwardly show no signs of concern.

Brad figures out where we are on the map and where Marble Canyon is. We park the van and load up our backpacks. We have dropped about 1,500 feet in elevation from the pass near Hunter Mountain, and the sun is warming us. Brad has done a good job with the map, and from this broad and rather flat area we find the top of the canyon and start down.

The canyon transitions from wide and gentle to narrow, rocky, and interesting. Upper Marble Canyon has several springs, but it is not too difficult to negotiate the plant life. There are some easy falls to descend, and we continue for a few miles until the canyon broadens out to a hundred feet across and there is a wide, sandy bench above the stream bed that is custom-made for us. The canyon walls are steep and, especially this deep in the winter, the area is shady and cool. On this first day we find a dead tarantula but no other animal life except small birds. The hiking is not too arduous, although I have not upgraded my backpack. It's heavy, of course, and there is again damage being done to my body by the shoulder and hip pads. I wasn't sure that these overnight adventures would continue, and the memory of the bruises faded too quickly. I am now certain that next year will feature a new pack on my back. We don't have any problem with water, partially because we have brought plenty and also because it is cool enough for us to drink less.

Speaking of being cooler, that means that the night is colder as well. I am just short of completely miserable in my sleeping bag when Johnny comes to my rescue again. He has some chemically activated hot packs and gives me one. Oh, what a miraculous invention! It is hard to believe that such a little heat source can make such a giant difference in comfort. I decide that I have to get some of these (along with the new backpack) after we survive this adventure.

In the morning, we get moving for today's semi-ambitious hike. Our goal is to descend a few more miles down Marble Canyon until we hopefully recognize where Deadhorse Canyon is and then hike Deadhorse to the top, several more miles away. The morning goes as planned, with us getting through several vegetated spring areas and the beautiful narrows near the confluence of the two canyons. We can see where we are relative to last year's hike, and it is easy to understand how we thought that Deadhorse Canyon was the main route, because the view from below these narrows almost hides the continuation of Marble Canyon. There is an advantage for us following up only a year later, since memories get foggier and dissipate with time. For example, I had quickly forgotten just how uncomfortable my backpack is.

A DV resident whose last walk did not end well

Up Deadhorse Canyon we chug, seeing the same bighorn sheep bones that we marveled over last year. Everything is pretty familiar, except the falls this year are not icy. That's a very good sign, since we plan to camp at a higher elevation. It's also a lot easier to climb falls without ice on them.

The top of the canyon opens to the high prairie whose location had us baffled last year. There are no live horses in sight today. Virtually the entire prairie is suitable for a campsite, so we plop down and call it home for the night. It has been a successful day, not getting lost, being in scenic canyons, and achieving our distance goal. There is a beautiful sunset in the clouds as the evening chill sets in. Happily, it doesn't look like rain.

The sunrise is just as beautiful. We have to cross-country trek on irregular terrain to find our way back to the car, and it involves some ravines and crossing Shorty Harris Canyon, which isn't very deep up here. It is only a few miles to travel, and Brad's orienteering proves accurate.

So, we do find our way back to the vehicle. As is usually the case with modern cars, it starts reliably. The last couple of days have been sunny and warmer, so the climb out of the canyon is without trauma. The remaining snow is soon behind us, so we take the cables off the tires. We get up and over the pass without incident. Nothing that I had quietly fretted about happens.

There is only one practical way out, which is back the way we came. It's amazing how much more relaxed and comfortable the drive is now, once we are down from the Hunter Mountain and South Pass area. With time on our hands and warmer weather, we make a couple of stops at mines we spot along the way. We climb down inside some openings into shallow holes but decline to enter the deeper ones. The road descends to about 3,000 feet, the elevation of a Joshua tree forest. Joshua trees are a beautiful decoration for this desert. The dirt road is well graded and it's easy driving to Highway 190.

Despite this trip's success, we did take some risks, vehicle-wise. I think that unless you are trying to prove something with solo travels, it is smarter to have a second vehicle in a remote location (or at least use one more suited to the application). Still, we have another unlikely success to talk about, and the minivan's moniker, "Johnny Quest," has been earned.

## Hiking Lessons

1. *Maps are good. Great work with the maps, Brad.*

2. *Since it now appears that I will be using it annually, I should invest in a modern backpack with shoulder and waist pads that haven't hardened to wood.*

3. *I will remember how cold the night was and get some of those magical chemically activated heat pads.*

## Life Lessons

1.  *Sometimes you just get lucky. Being careful will probably give you more chances at being lucky.*

2.  *In 1971, I rode an unreliable English motorcycle cross-country by myself. I brought tools and got to use them several times. The goodwill of people also saved me a few times. I was confident, but naïve and lucky then, as well—even more so. Have I learned a bit?*

3.  *A hundred years ago when motor vehicles were newly invented, all of the roads were dirt, and they got muddy when it rained or snowed. Those cars had slender, smooth tires with not much power to drive them. A lot of those cars got pulled out of ditches with horses. Our modern cars are definitely superior, even in the mud and snow.*

# Lemoigne

*Painful Lessons for the Stubborn*

The month leading up to this event is not my best and brightest. I over-extended myself on a ladder to trim a tree branch and slipped, and my gripping left hand got twisted and wedged, cracking bones. OK, that was really avoidable and stupid. The injury keeps me off bicycles, which are my main training mechanism. I also become a single-handed typist, but the good news is that my emails are now shorter and fewer. The staff at work is surely happy about that. It seems that my hand will be good enough to let me hike within a few weeks as long as I don't fall on it, so I continue to plan for the DVNP trip. Hey, I have a great new backpack that I need to try out.

Voni sometimes has premonitions. She warns me more than once that she has a bad sense about this trip and tells me not to go. I insist that my hand is good enough and that the latest weather forecasts predict clearing skies, so a flash flood or sleeping in the rain will not be risks. She thinks that maybe a mountain lion will find us, and I certainly can't outrun one of those. I tell her not to worry, because all I have to do is outrun John and Johnny. She doesn't laugh and knows that something will go very wrong. She also knows how stubborn I can be, and she reluctantly gives up. When it is time for the DVNP adventure, Voni and I drive from our new place in San Jose to Southern California, where she will spend a couple of days with friends and

I will meet up with the guys. She gives us four emergency medical kits just in case we do have a problem.

Our route this year begins with parking on descending Highway 190 along the east side of the Cottonwood Mountains at a roadside rest. We will hike several trailless miles across a large alluvial fan and then go several miles up Lemoigne Canyon, through narrows, to Lemoigne Mine. We have to trek across the alluvial fan by foot to the canyon mouth because the dirt road from Highway 190 to the canyon is one of the worst in DVNP, and Brad's minivan is highly unsuitable for that task.

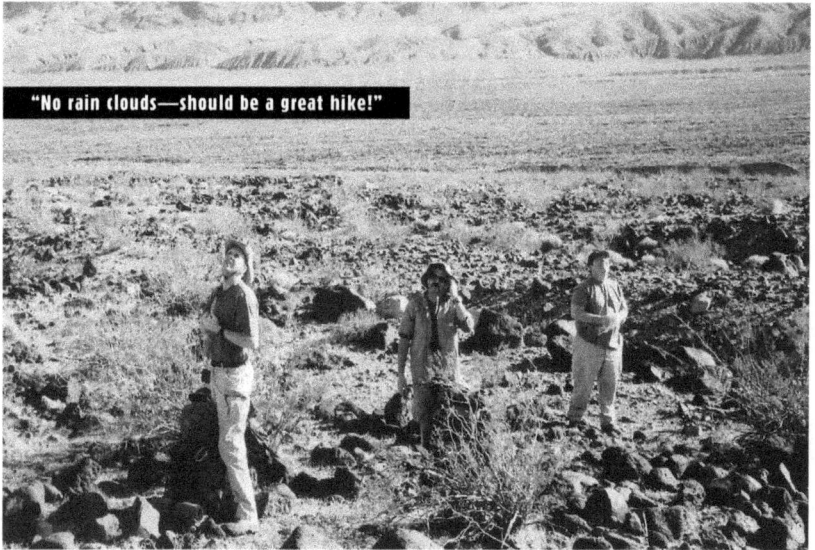

"No rain clouds—should be a great hike!"

Let's talk about alluvial fans. If you've seen desert mountain ranges from miles away, you've probably noticed that the big cracks high in the mountains have fan-like shapes that spill down from them, onto the slopes at the base of the mountain. Those smooth-looking fans are composed of alluvium, which just means eroded earthen debris.

Water and gravity are forever eroding mountains, with parts of the upper mountain dislodging from snow or rain. Those chunks are gradually broken by successive seasons of precipitation and more debris as water pushes and gravity pulls them further down. This angular stuff inexorably finds its way to the mouth of that crease or ravine on the side of the mountain, where the opening eventually widens. Here the water's energy is dissipated, and progressively smaller material drops to its temporary home until the next flood or rocks push it further and spread out the material. This fan of alluvium thus consists of a series of channels, each one periodically becoming clogged with deposited material, whereupon another set of channels forms as the water floods around the clog. Depending on the size of the mountain, these channels can be ten feet deep at the top of the fan and still several feet deep further down the fan.

Where adjoining fans spread out, given enough height and distance, they merge into a more even and less steep apron called a *bajada* that forms the base of the mountain. The channels near the top of a large bajada can still be a couple of feet deep. Often the bajada is punctuated with foothills or smaller subpeaks of the mountain range. Toward the base of the bajada, the channels may be gently broad and only a foot deep. The alluvial debris gets smaller and more rounded from abrasion as it is pushed and tumbles down to the mountain's base, until at the bajada the material can be mostly gravel and sand.

Alluvial fans and bajadas may appear to be surface features, but they can be thousands of feet deep. They are an elegant transitional morphology from uplifted mountain to the plains below that has infinite variety in execution.

Sometimes roads or trails will be constructed on alluvial fans as they make their way to a mountain pass, which is relatively easy construction because the surface is unconsolidated, and bulldozers can easily push around the material. Once it is crushed with more heavy equipment, the various sizes of sand, gravel, and rocks fit into each other and form a packed surface that's decent to build on. In human terms, the base is stable. In a geologic time frame, the road is destined to be destroyed by successive floods and its material will just become additional ingredients in the alluvial fan.

Sans road or trail, the loose alluvium on a bajada or alluvial fan makes for unstable footing. There is no easy path in any direction for any distance, but walking across it is the worst, because you have to continually climb and descend the channels. It would take an obsessive or foolish person to try and hike several miles across an alluvial fan. (You can see where this is going.)

From the minivan, we can see the opening for Lemoigne Canyon three or four miles west across the vast alluvial fan and without hesitation initiate our walk to it.

I still hike with running shoes, believing that I am young enough, athletic enough, and immune to the dangers posed to less capable persons who need to use heavy, expensive hiking boots that slow them down. Although

I've acquired hiking sticks, my left hand could get re-cracked by using them, so I'd decided not to bring them. I have a new backpack, finally, and figure that I should use it to carry a couple of gallons of water, because this trip does not have a spring anywhere along the route. The pack is quite heavy.

A logical person might reason that someone with a recently broken hand, no boots, a very heavy pack, and no walking sticks, who is not in his best physical condition because of that broken hand, would be unwise to make a traverse across a trailless alluvial fan. After three miles of up and down on unconsolidated steep slopes, we are getting fatigued. Just one more descent into this little arroyo, and we'll rest. My right foot slips, but I dare not fall on my left hand. I shift weight and the rock under my left foot gives way. I hear "crack, crack!" from my left leg and I crumble to the ground.

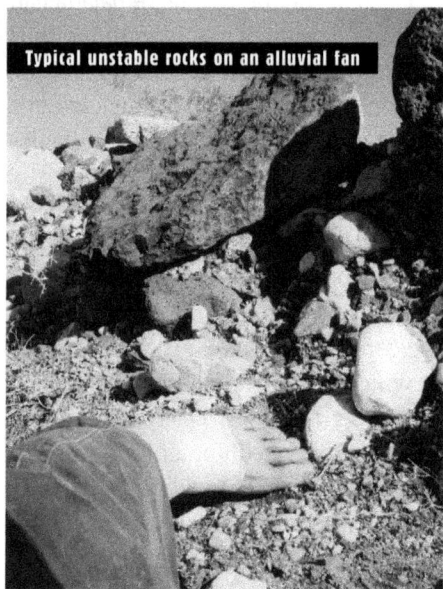

Typical unstable rocks on an alluvial fan

It's great to have a psychic wife but only if you are smart enough to pay attention to her.

Now is a good time to rest and take stock of the situation—as if we have a choice. Let's eat lunch! Oh, and let's find the ibuprofen in one of those medical bags that Voni gave us. Despite my now obviously foolish choices that led to this situation, I can help make a logical plan. Going further with a broken leg doesn't work, and it is way too far to crawl back to the minivan. There is no way they can carry me, and Johnny's walking sticks might serve as a crutch, but I don't know how bad the break is. Brad has our location on his GPS, so he can tell the rangers where I am. It looks to him that we may be close to the rough dirt road that leads into Lemoigne, but that's not where his car is, and it would be chancy to hope for anyone to be on that road. I am of no help in determining our location because topographic maps made for mountains are nearly useless on alluvial fans, since the endless furrows have less depth than the spacing of contour lines. According to a topographic map, alluvial fans are smooth expanses. Ha!

We decide that Johnny will stay with me while Doogie and Brad hike back to the van, drive to the ranger station, and hope that the rangers have a solution. That's the best we can come up with, but I don't know how they are going to get a helicopter here or what is going to happen after the rangers are notified. They might just laugh and say, "Good luck, suckers."

BJ and John dutifully head back across the hellish terrain from whence we came. Johnny looks really worried, and he does his best to make me comfortable with our sleeping bags. The ibuprofen that Voni provided in our medical kits is already coming in handy. The pain isn't too bad, but I shed tears because I ruined our vacation with my hubris—that excess of pride that killed many heroes in Greek tragedies.

The fluffy clouds are beautiful, and there isn't a lot to do but lie and watch them move and change shape. I'm in enough pain to keep me from being very social and I'm afraid to move much, not knowing the extent of the damage. I futilely try to figure out what to do next, but the best use of my energy would be to learn and reinforce useful lessons. Nah.

Hours pass. The sun is low. Johnny is worried because, well, nothing else has apparently happened. I assure him that we have food, water, and sleeping bags, so we'll be OK. Then Johnny is ecstatic to see a train of headlights moving up and down through the hills, coming toward us on a dirt road that we couldn't see. As it turns out, my friends went to the ranger station at Stovepipe Wells, and it seems that every ranger with an SUV has mobilized to come five miles up that impossible-to-traverse Lemoigne Canyon road.

With Brad's GPS coordinates, the rangers know exactly where to stop. By sheer amazing fortune, we are only about 200 yards from that road. Maybe God does protect the foolish. The rangers have come with a gurney that has one three-foot-tall rubber wheel in the middle and a hardy soul manning each corner handle. Wow, what a cool ride. They strap me down and push and pull over the rough landscape until we get to a Ford SUV. The rangers load us up and expertly get us back out on this challenging road. The ride in the gurney was less

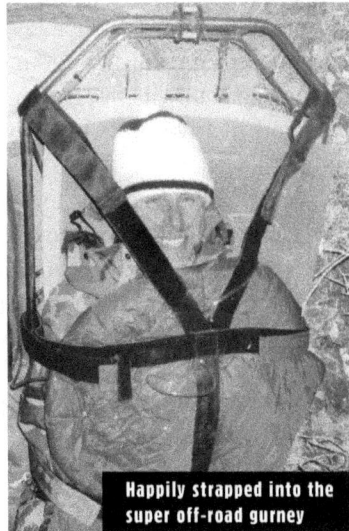

Happily strapped into the super off-road gurney

jarring and easier on my leg than this ride on the dirt road is, but I'm grateful to be treated to the car trip.

When we arrive at the ranger station it is completely dark, and my friends don't hesitate. We know there are no real medical facilities nearby, the pain is only a dull ache, and Ventura County is just five hours away. Back we go. In the town of Mojave, we stop at Mike's Café for dinner and my buddies prop me up as I one-leg in. It is a weird condition, trying to be thankful that we are all together and safe but also facing the reality that our annual trip has been torpedoed. I note that John and Johnny both order beers. At no time do my friends make me feel like I ruined things for them, although that is entirely true.

We are back where cell phones connect. I gamely call Voni, trying to sound exceedingly cheerful. She isn't fooled and instantly knows that something is wrong because cell phones don't work in Death Valley. She does not spend a lot of energy reminding me that she knew something bad would happen. For now, at least, she's glad that I'm alive and not mountain lion chow.

The guys finally get to their homes after dropping me off with my worried wife. They had no sleep the previous night and it is way past midnight, so they must be wiped out. Voni takes me to a Kaiser emergency room where they won't have a technician to x-ray me until 7:00 a.m., so I try to sleep on a bed in the ER while my poor wife shivers in our minivan in the parking lot for several hours. It turns out that I cracked a few bones in my foot and a one-inch section of bone in of my lower leg has broken away, completely severing the bone. I make lots of promises to be good, and they let me out with just a big medical boot and no cast. The irony: because I didn't wear hiking boots, now I have to wear a giant, clumsy ergo boot for two months. Voni gets to drive us six hours back to San Jose. Her little vacation has been ruined as well.

My coworkers can't believe that I've broken something else so soon after the broken hand. My boss no doubt has some second thoughts about having hired me. Our son is getting married the following weekend. My ex-wife gives me the stink eye, as if I had planned to break my leg before the wedding. Then again, maybe she knows me too well.

## Hiking Lessons

1.  *Sturdy hiking boots offer more traction and ankle protection than running shoes. Spend the money. Think of what you could save in*

*medical costs.*

2.  *Get walking sticks while at the store. They prevent falls, as will be proven on every future day of DVNP hiking. They are not for sissies; they are professional accessories for cool hikers.*

3.  *Don't hike in the wilderness alone. What became an interesting story could have been a life-threatening struggle if I'd been without my friends.*

## Life Lessons

1.  *If you are fortunate enough to know someone with the gift of premonition, suspend your logical doubts, then thank and pay attention to them when they warn you about something.*

2.  *Stubbornness and extreme personal pride are a dangerous combination. Get over them and get smarter.*

3.  *Most injuries in my life probably could have been avoided if I'd used more caution, had better equipment, or been smarter. I should wise up and learn that.*

4.  *Apologize to the people who have been tolerant with you despite how your personal shortcomings have caused them inconvenience, disappointment, and heartache.*

5.  *I am not as young and athletic as I think am. Maybe I was just luckier until now. In any case, don't be foolish with your life.*

# Lemoigne

*Do Over*

emoigne Canyon and Mine seemed like such a good idea last year, the group decides to try it again. This year, however, I am not able to be part of (enhance?) the adventure. Considering how it worked out last year, perhaps that is for the best. My wife doesn't have a bad premonition now, but I am sick with the flu. With the memory of 2005 still fresh enough, I am currently not so obstinate (in this one regard) as to think that being compromised and risking the vacation's success is a good idea. That's not to say that I've learned all of life's lessons or even learned many of them well. It just means that three good hikers can have a DVNP trip that is successful without me.

The report back is that they took the same route as we attempted last year. The narrows of the canyon are good, and the mines are extensive. Digonnet writes that Jean Lemoigne first made claims for lead and silver in this canyon in the 1880s, and he mined here as a solitary but reportedly quite congenial gentleman until his death in about 1919. Mining continued sporadically here, at times successfully, for the next sixty years. The guys find many adits (horizontal tunnels) and a few dilapidated structures to be cautiously explored. The dirt road in Lemoigne Canyon was used to transport ore out until the 1970s but has been essentially neglected since then, which is why it has degraded to a challenging four-wheel-drive route now. It doesn't rain often in Death Valley, but when it does, it can change the landscape and destroy dirt roads, especially in canyons and on alluvial fans. We will see plenty of evidence of that in future years.

Legends of "Old John" Lemoigne say that he loved this canyon and although educated in geology and literature, he mined apparently just enough to support his humble lifestyle and feed his mules. Being high enough in elevation to allow for a modest forest of Joshua trees, the area has a beauty for those who appreciate this type of scenery. It's good that the subsequent mining has ceased, returning quiet to the canyon for the few who explore it now. The scattered debris abandoned from the almost century of tunneled mining there adds a rustic décor that doesn't ruin the area if you bring an attitude of introspection. Modern-day strip mines totally demolish a landscape essentially forever, at least in human terms, and nobody goes to strip mines to enjoy the scenery.

I get through 2006 with various trips and adventures with Voni, including the wedding of a daughter in Idaho and visits to Bryce and Zion National Parks on the return trip. The Tour of California bike race comes through San Jose, which is great to experience. I hope that next year I will still be considered as a partner in the annual DVNP exploration. Spoiler alert: the book does not end here, so the group adventures do continue.

## Hiking Lessons

1. *If you can't bring something good to a hike with friends, don't go. The flu is a bad thing.*

## Life Lessons

1. *There are still activities that are interesting and valuable even if your anticipated special activity can't come to pass. Maybe that extends to things other than an annual DVNP hike.*

## 2007

# Cottonwood Canyon

*Getting Creatively Lost (Again)*

We are returning to the Cottonwood Mountains in the north Panamint Range, the closest ones to DVNP's southwest entry and the first one we approach from Ventura County. We have yet to explore all of the interesting places that Digonnet describes in this range, so here we are again. We haven't seen Cottonwood Canyon, which is just to the south of Marble Canyon and near Lemoigne Canyon. Brad's proposed access to Cottonwood Canyon from the top seems like an interesting hike. I'm pleased that my friends have included me this year on another adventure. Maybe I can be an asset rather than a liability.

I'm driving alone from San Jose and meet the other three at Furnace Creek to get a permit at the ranger station and have a last real meal. John presents me with a copy of *Hiking Death Valley*, which moves me because it means that I'm a full-fledged member of the group. I am excited to see my buddies and once again be part of the experience. From Furnace Creek, we backtrack west on Highway 190 and then go north for many miles on some paved and, eventually, dirt roads. These roads were scarier a few years ago in the snow but aren't that tough without snow. Fortunately, Brad is good with directions again and gets us to the top of Cottonwood Canyon, which is a few miles short of Marble Canyon. We park his minivan and my demi-SUV at about 5,000' elevation. We've seen no other vehicles on the dirt road and there are no other vehicles stopped here. It has taken a few hours to get this far, so it is late morning before we begin hiking. It's exciting to resume our annual adventure!

The plan is to trek down the upper reaches and springs of Cottonwood Canyon for about four miles, then explore the narrows in the lower part of the canyon. At some point, we'll camp and then either take this canyon back to the top or instead take a smaller, unnamed canyon to the north and then find our way back along the dirt road where the vehicles are.

Things seem simple when you summarize it like this. Digonnet mentions the gushing spring at the top of Cottonwood Canyon with a "brush-choked stream" and "thick undergrowth" in the upper part of the canyon. When Michel Digonnet mentions obstacles of any type, we are beginning to learn, it means that they could be something significant.

At least I start out blissfully unaware, not yet having opened my copy of *Hiking Death Valley*. We find our way to the head of Cottonwood Canyon— no problem so far. Early in the trailless canyon hike, though, we encounter thick brush. This is something unusual for DVNP. John and Johnny are both wearing shorts, but they follow where Brad and I lead with our long pants. It's not that they have much choice, but their legs are getting heavily scratched. It is especially hard to bushwhack with our large backpacks, so the going is slow—very slow. We rarely see any water because the springs are covered with dense growth. I'm sure that many species of bugs and smaller vertebrate animals are delighted to call this oasis canyon home. We, however, are bipeds who have come to DVNP to walk in the presence of naked rocks, not push our way through a jungle of scrubby plants that all seem to feature thorns.

Notice that I'm no botanist. I had to quit botany class after three weeks because trying to memorize all those genuses and species was impossible for my brain, and the effort was causing me to fail my other six classes, none of which required extensive memorizing. I have learned to recognize thorns, though.

I think Digonnet's fitness and experience level, significantly higher than the average hiker, mean that his descriptions are less intimidating than they would be if someone like me had written them. I'm certain that he's not deliberately being dismissive. Another very likely reason for a different description of some conditions is that his book was published in 1999, and it certainly would have taken him many years to hike and explore all of Death Valley. Many of the descriptions must be from a decade or more ago. As we will learn even more as our years of exploring DVNP continue, canyons in Death Valley get extensively cleared by periodic thunderstorm-fed flash floods. What one sees soon after a flood can be significantly different than it would be after years of accumulated brush growth and the modest flow patterns from the typical smaller rain events and ephemeral springs.

We give up trying to stay on the wash floor and find it to be somewhat better going on the slopes, above the thickest of the brush. Our route follows what could be the trails of wild burros. For us, this is a path of desperation.

In this manner the hours accrue, and we haven't even gotten past the spring-fed thickets. By midafternoon we collectively admit that at this rate we won't get down-canyon today to hit our target of the narrows or confluence with the next canyon to the north. John and Johnny may also bleed to death from the hundreds of scratches on their legs. We rest, and Brad lets me study the topo map. I think I see where we are on the map, only a couple of miles from where we started. None of us wants to concede complete defeat and backtrack through the brush to where we started, and this area does not have a good camp spot. Digonnet says that there are at least three springs in this canyon, but for the thick brush we don't know where the springs are or if we've encountered one, two, or three of them.

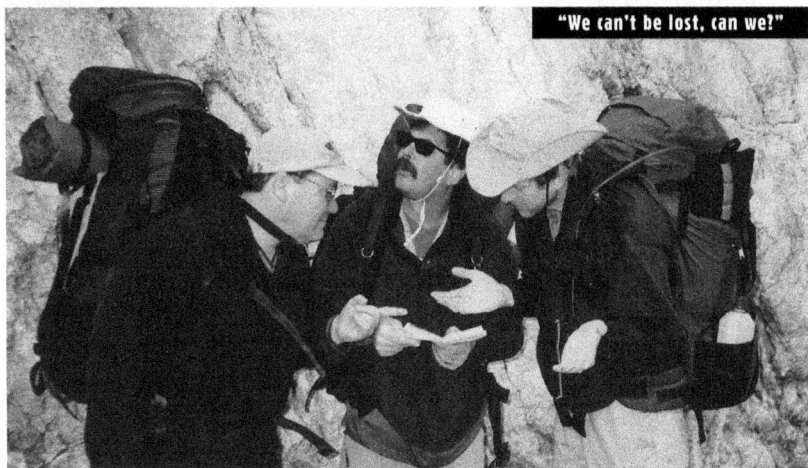

"We can't be lost, can we?"

On the map and across the canyon to the north, I can see a saddle maybe half a mile away and a few hundred feet higher. From various other hikes, I remember that a saddle on a ridgeline is often rather gently sloped and clear. It's called a saddle because the topography slopes down on both sides of the ridge but also goes up on the opposite ends—like a saddle for a horse. A saddle is often a pass over a ridge. Hoping that this saddle will be friendly and that it is also a way to the next canyon to the north, I propose we head there for the night. Brad's eyes light with enthusiasm for a new adventure. John and Johnny look resigned but hopeful—the kind of look you see in your dog's eyes when she pleads for her time at the veterinarian's office to be done.

Being emboldened and believing that the team needs to think that some-one has a plan and confidence, I take the lead. This is my idea to make work or fail, right? We crash through more brush and come to a shelf that extends a couple hundred feet along this south canyon side, about forty feet above the floor. This shelf is at best two feet wide, with a sheer wall above and below it. Maybe burros did use this path, but they didn't have packs and they had four feet for traction. There is really no other choice if we are going to move forward, so I sidle along, facing the wall for handholds, acting as if this is exactly what I'd planned. The footing is solid, as long as we don't lose our nerve or get pulled backward by the weight of our packs. I make a mental note to complain to the rangers about the lack of guard rails in these canyons.

It is with great relief that I see my friends moving surely behind me. Later that evening, John says that he only took that route because I had done so, and he was scared the whole way. I'm apparently just as much a culprit at putting us into compromising situations as I am in getting us out of some. That's not the type of character that everyone would call a friend on this kind of vacation.

Next we have to cross the canyon to get to the north side, so I do my best to push a path through the brush in what seems like the most permissive route. Again, three hardy and trusting souls are in my wake. We are now two-thirds of the way there. I take an angle up the canyon's slope, energized with an unreasonable amount of hope, and scramble on all fours for twenty minutes to the top. They aren't far behind, and we all summit as the sun is setting.

We can hardly believe it. The saddle is broad, smooth, and large enough for us all to bed for the night. We are beyond words. It's not the kind of joy that happens if you have won the World Series; it is more like the relief after some sort of grim battle is finished. Pads and bags are laid out, and our freeze-dried dinners seem particularly delicious.

Saddles can often be extremely windy, but the wind direction tonight is not over this ridge. Luckily, it seems as if the breeze tonight is down-canyon, also a common condition. So, it is not windy, the sky is clear, and the tem-perature at about 4,300' elevation is pleasant. I awake face-up hours later and see two large dark birds silently soaring directly above, blocking the stars as they glide over this saddle. I'm without my glasses, so I assume that they are either ravens or great horned owls. Ravens don't usually fly at night, and they have wings that make a bit of a whoosh. Owls hunt at night and have silencing feathers so that they can sneak up on prey. Perhaps these are the first owls any of us sees in DVNP, however unclearly. In any case, the image will stay with me forever.

In the morning, the conditions are still comfortable, and we see that our campsite has a fine view of both canyons. Marble Canyon has brush as far as we can see in both directions, and the unnamed canyon to the north is clear, free of springs and that green thorny stuff (that is my botanical description) that grows here. You can guess which one we decide to take.

The hike down to the more northern canyon floor is not as steep as the one climbing up to the ridge yesterday. Our extended walking sticks make the descent safe enough for us to not have to crawl down. We take an angle so as to intersect the wash further up-canyon and minimize the distance and elevation changes. After yesterday's forging through a jungle of brush and climbing up and down steep and unstable slopes, a dry wash seems like a dream to walk on. The canyon walls are not sheer, and the wash is rather broad, so we don't have much trouble finding an acceptable route. The canyon is a narrow v, and the scenery is attractive.

In a couple of miles, we get to the top of this canyon. We rather easily find the road that leads us back to the cars, only a mile away.

The hikes from some years have left us with a lot of fuzzy or even blank spots in our memories about what happened. All of the hikes, including this one, have also left us with some experiences that will forever be with us.

With accrued age, I have decidedly mixed feelings about the potential danger that we have sometimes sloughed off. We don't jump off cliffs into streams or descend into mines with rotted wooden ladders and unstable roofs, but we do seem to embrace some actions that others would regard as unnecessary or only marginally intelligent. Part of me says that without adventure there is no sauce in life, and adventure means taking calculated risks. Another part of me, the old guy telling this story, says that is an imma-ture and stupid attitude that can get people hurt or killed.

I seem to live in a sort of balance between the two extremes. It feels acceptable to ride a motorcycle and bicycle, but I always wear a helmet and don't try to find the limit of traction or trust every car driver with my life. It appears that Brad, Johnny, and John also embrace life somewhere around that edge of balance, at least during our DVNP trips. Brad would no doubt confirm with an enthusiastic yes. When I ask the other two guys, I'll try to gauge their real feelings by how diplomatically they word their replies. Well, at least they keep coming back for more, so perhaps that is answer enough.

## Hiking Lessons

1.  *Even in Death Valley, be cautious about committing to a hike in a well-watered canyon that almost nobody else with two legs regularly visits.*

2.  *Once you try a planned hike for a while, if it isn't working as well as you'd hoped, stop to reassess the situation. You may be able to devise an alternative while there is still time and energy.*

3.  *Choose hiking partners who have a similar tolerance for your level of adventure.*

## Life Lessons

1.  *Once you try anything for a while, if it isn't working as well as you'd hoped, stop to reassess the situation and devise an alternative while there is still time and energy.*

2.  *Choose a life partner who has a similar tolerance for your level of adventure.*

# 2008

# Goler Canyon, Warm Springs Canyon, & Butte Valley

*Let's Not Break the Truck*

The Panamint Mountains are the western north-south trending range of DVNP—the largest and tallest range here. They are where we have had all of our adventures until now, although we were more toward the northern part. This year, we will explore about sixty miles further south and do it differently. John's brother graciously (foolishly?) loans us his almost-new four-wheel-drive crew cab Chevy truck, which we will take across this mountain range on a primitive road. The truck is unblemished, appears to have stock wheels and tires, and is not lifted for more ground clearance. It does, however, have lots of room inside for four guys, and the bed easily swallows all of our backpacks. Any truck with four-wheel drive appears infinitely capable after all of our years of taking minivans down dirt roads.

I've driven down from San Jose to Lancaster, where Johnny lives. John and BJ arrive with the truck before sunrise. We load up our stuff and off we go to Ballarat, about three hours away.

Ballarat is essentially a ghost town (population < 5) outside the southwest portion of the park, and it is accessed from a six-mile-long graded dirt road. The much, much longer unmaintained dirt road south of Ballarat that goes into Goler Canyon and the park boundary requires four-wheel drive and high clearance and reportedly becomes ever more challenging as one climbs into the canyon narrows. Goler Canyon has earned legendary status in the four-wheel-drive community. It is, therefore, the perfect place to test someone else's near-new, stock truck.

Why the big shift this year from hiking a canyon to driving a long, rough dirt road? Because that is the only way for all four of us to see some peculiar things in the southern half of the Panamint range. There are no paved or even smooth dirt roads into this area, and there is just too much ground to cover for us to do it by foot. It is really a stroke of flexible genius for Brad and John to come up with this alternative DVNP adventure. This quadrant of the park is an area of well over 500 square miles that we can get the flavor of by taking this drive.

Goler Canyon is like other canyons in DVNP in that it is narrow with areas of gravel wash, areas of jumbled smooth limestone basement, and areas of small to large rocks. There are also several springs and, for some welcomed but unknown reason, no large and seriously steep falls. Because it is a narrow Death Valley canyon, if there ever was a trace of a road here it has long since been erased by flash floods.

We find out all of these facts within the first few miles after entering the canyon from the west side. None of us is an expert at four-wheeled off-roading, but Brad and I have mountain-biked our share and driven some less treacherous dirt roads in Death Valley with our minivans. Brad does the lion's share of the driving, while I jump out to scope sketchy spots that we approach. To be honest, part of my motivation is just nervous energy. There are places where I move some large rocks out of the way and other places where I put rocks into cavities. Sometimes Brad has to carry momentum to make it through a section, and at other times a crawl is the best approach.

We go past a couple of significant springs that would be delightful in hot weather, but today it is mild and pleasant. This process goes on for a couple of hours, with us making progress that averages only about two or three miles per hour, but without getting stuck or causing any damage to the truck. We're feeling pretty successful, and then we encounter a phalanx of very serious looking jeeps coming down the canyon and move aside for them. We are now wondering if continuing is the greatest idea, since these people have vehicles that can handle conditions much worse than we've encountered so far. We smile and wave, as if confident. We don't know if they are thinking, "Are these guys fools?" That could be true, because we continue, deciding to take this adventure as far as we can. It seems to be our way.

Since Brad can't see what is just in front of the truck because of the hood, at times I am walking backward in the lead, indicating where he might steer. He doesn't seem to mind and, again, I'm getting exercise and feeling somewhat useful. This morning has all been climbing, and we have ascended a few thousand feet in elevation. As we get into the afternoon, the truck is still completely intact.

Then we arrive at The Place.

Everyone gets out of the truck. Maybe if you have a short wheelbase jeep with lots of ground clearance and huge tires then this spot is not a problem, but that is not true for this rig. We have a little confidence because of our success so far, but this rocky climb is of a different scale. BJ and I think that if we move a fair number of rocks and Brad takes an exact path with some momentum and the truck is able to climb better than we have yet to ask it, *maybe* it won't get stuck. John and Johnny don't seem nearly as convinced, but they go along with helping to move rocks. Once again, Brad and I have gotten them into a situation where they have little choice but to go along, hoping that they have a happy story to relay when we return home. Fifteen minutes later, three of us stand aside, everyone takes a deep breath, and BJ guns it. Ten seconds of roaring engine and some tire spin and dramatic bounding later, and he has cleared the section.

We have to do something similar in a couple more places, but never again does it seem like we might fail. Are we just four lucky fools or some incredibly talented guys? Either assessment could be true.

By late afternoon, we clear the canyon and go through Mengel Pass at 4,330' elevation. We've gone about ten miles in the six or seven hours since we entered the canyon. That's a bit faster than we would have travelled if walking with a pack, and it would have been a tough uphill hike.

Going downhill now is easier because momentum allows us to slowly roll over obstacles that would have made climbing problematic. It occurs to me that those professional four-by-fours that we encountered earlier today had chosen the easier downhill route through Goler Canyon. Ha! We made it anyway.

The scenery opens up and we can see down into Butte Valley. This seems like a fine place to stop for the night, as there is a little wind protection and some decent spots to lay out our bags in an arroyo next to the road. Considering that we haven't had a lot of regular hiking exercise today, we are plenty tired, or maybe we are just adrenaline-exhausted. The night is beautiful with a full moon rising, and the elevation here is enough to add a significant chill to the air once the sun sets.

When we wake, there is frost on our sleeping bags. Having the cheapest bag, I slept with thermal underwear, shirt, pants, hat, gloves, and a jacket in my bag. I'm not frozen solid. The sun's warmth is welcomed. Now might be a good time to note that when the manufacturer of a sleeping bag says that it is good down to, say, 30 degrees, that means something other than what most people might think. It does NOT mean you'll sleep comfortably at 30 degrees; it just means that you won't freeze to death.

We don't have to pack quite as carefully because the load doesn't go on our backs. Nobody complains about these changes as we throw the stuff into the truck bed. The truck doesn't seem to be encumbered at all by the weight of our packs and bodies. It is almost as if it was designed for carrying things and people. Yeah, maybe it was.

The air is clear—the usual DVNP condition—and we can see for miles across the high Butte Valley. There is more vegetation up here at around 4,000' elevation, sparsely growing to about four feet high. A lot of it is healthy creosote, with many other plants that I can't name, being so botanically deficient. We enjoy the easy, slow roll across the landscape, aptly named

The wild burros seem pleased to see us.

because there are buttes (rocky outcrops) here and there. It occurs to me that this might be a place where wild burros could live. We've never seen them, but then we've never been in this type of country before. These burros are the descendants of the original miners' pack animals, and the park naturalists consider them to be an invasive species. To be truthful, they certainly are, but it would be nice to see some in case they are all appropriately removed. This thought has been with me for less than half an hour before I ask Brad to stop. We all climb out and, sure enough, a few hundred feet away there is a small herd of burros. Their coloration and short height make them extremely well camouflaged in this high desert brush, although nothing other than men would ever hunt them here. We spread out to try and flank them and get closer, but the burros don't fall for our ploy. We never get less than about 150 feet from them. Still, it feels like a satisfying success.

In a rocky side canyon, we find a cluster of attached steel-roofed bare-wood buildings, still standing but looking like they could fall at any time. It's not clear where the mine or other activity that supported this venture was. A few miles later, we encounter another building that had been a decent-sized house, with the walls and roof intact. It is also unclear why someone had decided to live here, aside from the fact that the view is great, overlooking some low hills to a mountain range beyond. There must have been water here somehow, because one large, but now dead, tree stands near the front porch. Dangling from the tree are an array of automotive and other assorted steel mechanical parts that Johnny admires. It's a wind chime, Death Valley style. This home was somebody's pride and joy, abandoned now for at least fifty years. Nearby are the rusted remains of a 1920s-era auto with the top sawed off. BJ climbs into the driver's seat and squints as if looking for a path, while John sits in the back seat with a map unfolded, pointing directions. It makes for a good photo.

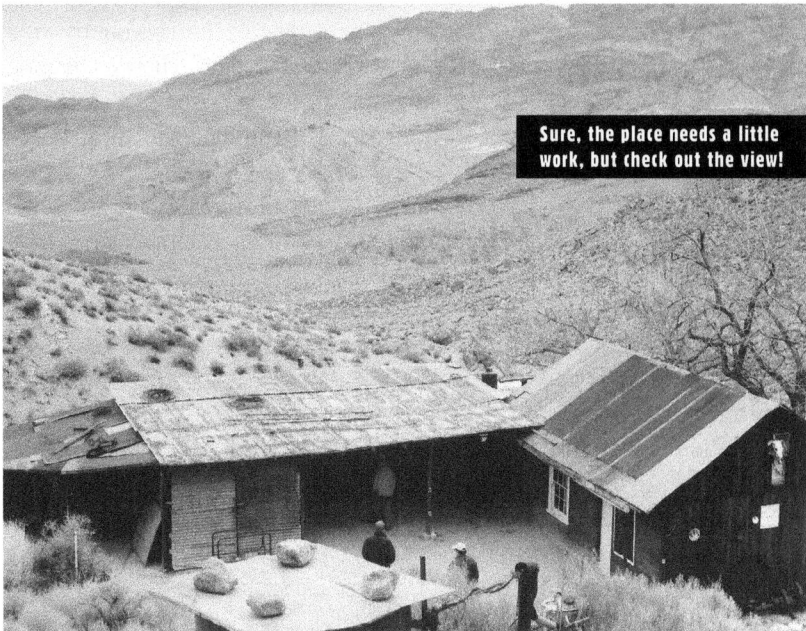

Sure, the place needs a little work, but check out the view!

There are more beautiful vistas, and no other operational vehicles are encountered. We decide to stop for lunch on a butte, and we climb up to the rocks on the crest to enjoy our meal. By our standards it has been a bit of a cheat to get here by truck, but the relaxing lunch break and broad views are somehow not diminished in quality.

There are few intersections with this dirt road. It has taken us east through Goler Canyon, north through Butte Valley, and then east through Warm Springs Canyon. Warm Springs Canyon is not challenging, and we gradually descend to the Warm Springs camp and various talc mines. There is a thick and extensive layer of talc here that is exposed along the hillside, and several mines tunnel into it from this valley.

The talc deposits were pure and rich enough to support mining here for many decades. Digonnet writes that Louise Grantham and Ernest Huhn located claims here in the 1930s. Mining was continuous from the 1940s until the 1950s, when diesel equipment and better ventilation was introduced, and was still profitable in this lower canyon until the 1970s. Further up the canyon, a later strip mine exposed this rich deposit hundreds of feet below the surface. That mine produced over $5 million of product until the late 1980s and was one of the last active mines in Death Valley. We consider all of the frantic activity that took place across Death Valley, with dozens of mines started and fortunes lost seeking silver and gold. It turns out that the only sustained profitable ventures here were mining talc and borax, common minerals used in cheap household products. Now that's ironic.

We climb around some still-standing steel loading facilities. The openings to the mines are wisely shuttered. We find our way to the Warm Springs camp. Still remaining are several decent buildings with tile floors, solid walls, and modern roofs. In what was a broad courtyard, there is a large concrete swimming pool, now backfilled with dirt. There are lush trees and the remnants of a garden area; a modest lined stream of warm water burbles down from the hill that is behind the house. This was the place that Louise Grantham built for herself and her workers. Wow, if you wanted to be a miner working away from the rest of society, she created a relative paradise to live in. She had running water, toilets, a pool, and electricity here. Leave it to a woman to make a fine living for herself and a bunch of men by mining talc in Death Valley. Sometimes it is embarrassing to be male.

In honor of Louise, we strip to our undies and tennis shoes, then hike up the hill to the reported rock pool where this spring originates. Yes! It is warm water as fine as any hot tub, deep enough to slouch down and get sub-

merged. This is our first
and it turns out our only
hot bath that we would
ever have in Death Valley.

Back down, clothed
and inside the build-
ing, we create our usual
dinner fare. It feels a bit
surreal to be this far from
anything else resembling
a town, in the place where
someone created real civi-

Luxuriating in a rustic hot tub.

lization sixty years ago and kept it going for a long time. We do have to admit
that the floor is cold and hard, so we all opt to lay our bedding outside, under
the well watered trees. It is a lot more comfortable here than last night, as
we are down to 2,400' elevation. Maybe the protection of the large trees or
the residual heat of the spring help, but we surely sleep warmer tonight.

In the morning after breakfast and packing, we poke around the mines
some more. We finally load our packs onto our backs and hike a mile to the
north, away from the spring. It is barren and rocky here at the southeast
base of the mountains. Our destination is the Pink Elephant Mine, which
was for fluorite. Digonnet reports that the gneiss here is 1.7 billion years
old—the oldest rocks in DVNP and the basement of the Panamint Range.
There are still a lot of wooden remains of mining structures and one open
adit, which we walk into for a while until our nerves cause us to exit. It
feels good to be walking more, and we do much of our exploring without
the heavy packs. We spend the day poking around and then find a somewhat protected spot in the wash that is more hospitable to laying out our
bedding. It has not been a tough day of hiking, but it feels more like our
traditional DVNP adventure because we carried our packs into this location.
The night is pleasant.

In the morning, we know that it is a short hike out of this canyon to
the truck, so we search for an activity that gives the day another memory.
Above us, the hill rises for a few hundred feet at a steep but not completely
intimidating angle to what looks like a saddle. We agree to climb that hill
without packs and take in the view before calling an end to our adventure.
It turns out that the climb is a bit challenging, but the deep breathing and
panoramic view make the effort cleansing and rewarding. Nobody gets hurt

on the way down either. We then heave on our packs and tromp downhill for a mile or so to the truck.

The dirt road east from Warm Springs Canyon becomes much smoother for fifteen miles as it descends the alluvial fan down to the floor of Death Valley, below sea level. We are on Badwater Road in less than an hour. It will take another two hours to exit DVNP on Highway 190 on the west side. Every moment is cherished as the views unfold and we savor our recent experiences. As is often the case with our gender, not a lot is said, but much is felt.

Despite the challenging conditions and all of the opportunities to pound the truck's underside or doors on some rocks, we have managed not to do any of that. Although dusty, the truck appears to have sustained no damage. It carries us home smoothly and quietly, without any disconcerting noises. It took us to see lots of wild country, abandoned ruins, deserted mines, and burros—and to do some back-country hiking.

Between our caution, the prayers of Johnny and John, Brad's driving skills, and the competency of the truck, we are able to return this vehicle with proud tales of its ability and no shame about damaging it. That outcome might have been unreasonable to expect when we entered Goler Canyon, and I believe that the line of professional four-by-four jeepsters we met would have bet against us.

## Hiking Lessons

1.  *You don't have to hike everywhere.*

2.  *Once you carry your pack into a destination, you don't have to wear it while you explore. Nobody else is around to poke inside your stuff.*

## Life Lessons

1.  *Sometimes to achieve a goal, e.g., seeing much of DVNP, you have to change methods.*

2.  *Can we make a Chevy truck commercial? For all I know, though, all modern trucks are this competent. The Ford SUVs that rescued me from Lemoigne were pretty amazing too.*

3.  *Raise a glass to toast Louise Grantham, a pioneer in women's intellectual power and drive.*

# Ashford Canyon

*Don't Go in That Mine*

This year, we decide to explore some mines in the Black Mountains, which run north-south along the southeast border of DVNP. We access Ashford Canyon at the southern end of Badwater Road near where it joins Highway 178 and enter Death Valley from the southeast. Along the south end of Badwater Road, we see a sign for the nearby Ashford Mill Ruins on the west; across from it, to the east, we take a 2.8-mile rough dirt road that climbs up the alluvial fan and ends near the opening of Ashford Canyon. The road gets progressively worse, and we park a ways before the road is erased at the canyon's wash.

We pack up for a few days in the wild and follow the remnants of the Ashford Canyon road, which starts on the north flank of Ashford Canyon. Digonnet reports that down in the canyon there are several falls, and for the sake of time and lowering our risk of misadventure, we choose not to take that route. It is strange for us to be following the course of a road, although there are only portions of it that still resemble a road. This hike is only a few miles long and without a lot of elevation gain, but our trek would be a lot more challenging if the original miners hadn't built this road to take their ore down to Ashford Mill. We let discretion be our guide in this case, having heavy packs and, except in BJ's case, only average climbing skills. The road is discontinuous, but its basic direction is clear enough.

On the way up to the main camp, we see a few mine adits to walk into that show no significant degradation, so they seem perfectly safe to explore. Well, safe from collapse at least.

We turn on our headlamps and walk into a dry adit on a hillside. It is about ten feet wide and flat, and it goes in for about a hundred feet. At the end of this length, it makes a hard left turn. For some reason, it feels a little strange here and we have a premonition that something isn't right, but it still looks OK. We make the turn and go a little way further; then, near the end of the tunnel, our lamps light up a pile of bighorn sheep bones. We all freeze. That sheep didn't come in here to die, it was dragged in here by a mountain lion. There is no lion now—we can imagine the panic if we'd trapped it here. Not wanting to wait for a return and with few words, we turn around and hustle out. Four grown men afraid of a cat. It still seems reasonable.

Being suddenly cured of any desire to explore more adits, we make good time on the rest of the walk up the canyon to the main mine camp. The area is rich with mines and rough structures left from the first half of the twentieth century. There are plenty of places for us to explore and get a feel for the life of miners eighty years ago. Some mine openings look structurally sound and appear impractical as cat lairs, so we cautiously go into a few. Most of our time is spent poking around the residential and office structures. All are rough wood and some still have their corrugated steel roofs. We are finally content with the day's excitement, and we settle down for the evening. As always, rehydrated freeze-dried dinners seem like gourmet fare in these settings with no food or water resources other than what we haul in.

In the morning, Brad suggests that we take a day-hike adventure to one of the local overlooks that Digonnet has written about. We're all up for almost anything that involves not carrying our heavy packs. It is only a mile or so to the top, but still an interesting walk and a good place for lunch. We seem to never get enough of the Death Valley panoramas, with every canyon having its own colors and curves. We four work hard to attain what we consider these peak experiences for a short period on an annual basis, but I can imagine how miners could have tired of this if it was their everyday reality. More common statements then might have been, "Is there no end to these desolate, barren stretches?", "What a God-forsaken landscape!", and "If I ever get out of here, I swear to never return."

It is interesting how one's life experiences and personality can shape perspective. For me, I can tolerate dense cities only temporarily. The streets, walls of buildings, flat sameness, and zombie throngs of humanity deaden my life spirit in a few days. I end up depressed and inexplicably frantic. This explains why I live in places walking or biking distance from natural refuges. My wife understands it but doesn't feel it.

We return to our packs, which represent home. That is another interesting perspective: that home is a backpack. This is something that works for us for a few days because we have the conveniences and comfort of modern life for the rest of the time. Decades ago, I lived with nothing more than a motorcycle or bike and a backpack for weeks at a time. It finally cured me of any notion of spending my whole life that way, and I eventually settled into a stable dedication to my wife and school studies. Now I'm scarred with the realization that my personality needed to get that lesson hammered into me repeatedly, whereas most people seemingly never require such instruction. Well, maybe a lot of soldiers and sailors and the miners who used to live here got that lesson. Perhaps they became better—or at least more settled—people for the experience. I've decided that men are more than a little stupid and crazy at times. For some reason, a few people, guys mostly, get the genetics that make them restless, probing outside the edges of their environment. Science has proven that we all end up dead anyway. History has shown that a lot of women have paid a high price for loving men infested with this behavior.

So, we get another quiet evening and night in a place that we find to be novel and interesting. As always, the conversation is good because the three other guys are well read, thoughtful, candid, honest, and engaging. No electronic devices, phones, or responsibilities intrude on us. Civilization has given us knowledge and ideas to share, but in our lives we usually have little energy or time to do so. In the evenings we modern men usually quietly watch TV, where the fantasy adventures of others are acted out for us. I believe that we achieve more bonding in a couple of nights camping than would happen in a year of evenings in front of a television.

The next day, we pack up and head back down the canyon the way we came in. It is typical DVNP—scenic and so unlike where we spend the rest of our lives. As with most of our trips, we have encountered nobody else this entire time. If we didn't have each other for company and security, that might be unnerving. For us, it seems perfect and just what we hope for.

The last day is always a combination of sadness to be leaving and excitement for more adventure on the way out, culminating in the comforts of civilization. The path and broken road down to the cars seem somewhat familiar but strange to me, with a haunting memory that I can't articulate, and it lasts for years. Johnny reveals to me later that he had nightmares in the

Ashford Mine camp. Some people are much more in tune with the paranormal, whereas most of us are either completely unaware or just dismissive about such things. You can categorize me as a believer but not jealous of the ability. I'm haunted enough with the specters of my own creation.

We load up the cars and head out. My friends all still live in Southern California, and I am now in San Jose. We take the same roads as far as Mojave, where Mike's Restaurant is our usual final road meal and place where we split. Mike's has fine coffee-shop fare and is decorated with fun stuff from the fifties and sixties. They also tolerate us, because I'm not sure that we look or smell so great at this point. It is a good reintroduction to society from a place that has a bit of pioneer desert feel. It is a couple of hours more driving from here for my friends and about six for me. I have a Honda del Sol, a little convertible with character, making the most of my journey. Coming to DVNP is worth it, but it's a long schlep to and fro between there and San Jose.

## Hiking Lessons

1.  *I'm not sure if this is a lesson that carries to very many places but be careful in old adits because they might harbor a mountain lion.*

## Life Lessons

1.  *Be happy that we get to take hiking trips as a diversion to regular life and be appreciative of the comforts of modern life and a good spouse. Don't take either for granted.*

2.  *If you are seriously infected with wanderlust, unless your spouse is similarly afflicted, try to address the worst of it before committing to a mate.*

3.  *Just because you don't experience ghosts doesn't mean they aren't real. Maybe some spirits don't die contented and don't get to rest in peace. I feel sorry for them and wish I could help, and I wish I could better understand the afterlife.*

4.  *Check to make sure that the film is properly advancing in your camera or you might one day end up writing a book with a photo-free chapter*

# 2010

# Virgin Spring Canyon & Desert Hound Mine

## *What's Virgin about Here?*

This year, Brad has called us back to the Black Mountains, to a canyon just east of last year's hike. The idea of traipsing up an empty canyon to see abandoned mines felt extremely Death Valley-like last year, and it seems that we haven't gotten our fill of it. At this point in our lives, we still feel young and adventurous enough to be many miles from any road in places where very few people since the miners of a hundred years ago have visited. It is fortunate for people like us that Digonnet has explored the area and left us with directions. We were raised and live in predictably safe and comfortable surroundings, so these few days skirting that security feels daring, even if that is only partly true.

This year, there is a new member accompanying us. Chris is similar to BJ in build, age, fitness, and desire for adventure. He comes to us with all of the appropriate modern equipment—something that I didn't begin with. That makes him wiser or smarter than me, for starters. A lot of the lessons from these adventures, many not learned until I write about them, are humbling. I choose to believe that at least it is better to eventually recognize, learn, and grow than never to do so. I hope that others do not have to struggle similarly.

The weather is sunny and gets into the 70s each day, something common for DVNP's lower elevations in the winter and always welcomed. For most people who live elsewhere in the United States, that must seem like impossibly pleasant conditions for early January, but everyone knows the trade-off when the summer comes to Death Valley.

We have our usual meeting at Furnace Creek for back-country permits, a hearty breakfast, and the use of facilities supplied with running water. Next we travel east on Highway 190 and then south for about twenty-five miles on Highway 178 before heading up a dirt road for less than a mile and parking when the road gets tough. We've again managed to start a DVNP hike after less than thirty miles of driving from our initial meeting point. Considering the vastness of this place, that is not much added travel.

A casual observer would see five guys piling out of two cars in the middle of nowhere and probably conclude that we must have mutual insanity. We are a couple of miles from the mountains with no modern landmarks; there are no other vehicles, and there is no apparent reason why we have collectively decided that this is the place to stop and leave our perfectly functional transportation. To tell this observer that we have old directions and a rough map to a destination in an even more remote place where nobody lives and there are no conveniences, including a promise of three nights sleeping on the ground, would only serve to confirm to the observer that we really are loony. As I write this, I realize that there are legitimate alternate perspectives to what makes sense, at least in this case.

So, we do our familiar routine. The packs are heavy with water, as we don't have any promise of finding significant water for three days. We start here at 1,200' elevation and cheerfully walk uphill northeast along the approximate alignment of a dirt road virtually erased by a flood that came down Virgin Spring Canyon some years ago. In about a mile we see to the north, another mile away, what we think is the opening to Virgin Spring Canyon. This is not a dramatically narrow vertical-sided canyon like those featured in some previous hikes. It is several hundred feet wide in the wash, and the walls rise about 1000 feet. It takes a few thousand horizontal feet for the sides to climb that high. From our perspective, these mountains are mostly just brown, unspectacular rock. Digonnet gives an exquisite geological perspective of this canyon, clearly indicating that he is a more attentive and skilled geologist than I. For us today, just finding our way up the wash takes all of our energy.

Being a dry wash, the surface is not dangerous for footing or as highly channeled as an alluvial fan, but it also is not hard, smooth, and straight.

After about three miles of this walking, we look for the faint drainage to the west that Digonnet says will lead us to Virgin Spring and then the lower trail to Desert Hound Mine. There has been no trail so far, but he says that off to our west above the spring there is a ridge with a trail to the mine that traces from about 2400' to 4000' elevation for another three miles. We think we see this connection and find the spring, such as it is. Digonnet says that Virgin Spring yields only about ten drops per second, but what we find is completely dry. I suggest that the larger drainage to the north is an easier geographic feature to follow, so we take it. This seems to work OK for us, five guys with significantly lower levels of mapping skills than our prophet.

Virgin Spring seems well named.

This unnamed stream bed is friendly enough, with a sandy bottom and not many rocks or brush. In another mile we decide that we have had plenty of this fun for the day. We are at about 3,300' elevation, and it is shadier and cooler than where we started. The sand will make for a good bed surface. The gentle walls indicate that this drainage will peter out pretty soon, meaning that campsites may not be as favorable if we keep walking and the wash ends.

Hopefully we'll be able to see the trace of the old trail tomorrow morning when we climb to the end of this drainage—assuming we're not lost. Being lost is always a possibility. When we've experienced that before, we have sometimes employed the option to turn around and go back downhill. We don't expose our getting-lost percentages to our latest member, Chris. We just declare, "Hey, this is a fine place to camp, isn't it!" and leave it at that. No need to add drama and worries to the situation, and Chris might still think that we know what we're doing.

Although the hike has been uphill and trailless with heavy packs, we aren't totally exhausted because the distance has only been about four miles. Still, because the night before our first day's hike is usually without much sleep, we welcome the stop. In my photos of this spot, there are guys proudly displaying their sleeping bags and gear spread in the sand. It is, again, one of those situations where other people might logically think that we are de-ranged. From our perspective, though, this is quite comfortable. The weather is pleasant, and we have all we need at this stage of our adventure. Our night under the stars passes well.

The next morning, we know that to make our way efficiently to Desert Hound Mine, we really should find the lower trail. We will soon be leaving this drainage, and there is no canyon to follow up to the mine, as it is perched at about 4,000' elevation in a bunch of hills and ridges. Maybe we have been deceiving ourselves thinking we can hike anywhere without trails, when realistically it *usually* isn't so hard to find your way when you simply walk up a canyon. This time it is different—we could really use a trail. The 200' contour lines on the topographic map don't show these hills and less distinctive features at all, so we could be lost. Again, we don't reveal any of this to Chris. The blissfully unaware man might still believe that he is with competent adventurers.

It is encouraging that we climb out of this wash in another half mile, indicating that we could be where we thought we were on the map. We scout around, and voila, there is a trace of a trail that goes west. It is a happy moment.

As Digonnet warned, this lower trail is sketchy in definition and sometimes steep. In order to keep us seemingly making progress, we use a compass to find west, identify features in that direction, and keep heading that way. As we reach each set of features, we have to stop and repeat that process. The walking surface on weathered hilltops and ridges is usually smooth, as it is in this area. Without a lot of traffic, though, a trail can get erased in many places, as is also true here. There is no shade, but it is comfortable short-sleeve weather, so we aren't using our water too quickly. In a mile or so, we are up to 4,000' elevation, where we find a much better-defined trail continuing west and back to the northeast.

According to our maps, this is the Desert Hound Trail. Wow—Brad and I actually got us where we intended! The other three guys smile their con-gratulations, at least as relieved as we are that being lost isn't part of the experience so far. Perhaps this is their first realization that we had been unsure of ourselves.

Going due west along the trail for another half mile leads us to the spectacular Desert Hound Mine. Spectacular? Now there are no buildings, a partially collapsed adit, and a pile of rusted steel cooking utensils and other things that were of insufficient value to carry away when the mine became too much effort for the return in gold.

According to Digonnet and other historians, Walter Scott, aka Death Valley Scotty, had been a charlatan and cheat, whose only semi-redeeming quality was his ability to spin yarns and sell dreams. Getting people to invest their money and time in this gold mine was a prime example of his work. Digonnet reports that a few miners did extract some gold from this place, but the extreme isolation and modest ore quality eventually took the life energy out of everyone who gave it a try. All that is left is what we see here. Oh, and the trail.

This was another chapter in the oft-repeated story of Death Valley. For five modern men who have now hiked here, it is educational to poke around the ruins and step a few feet inside the mine. The last mining effort was in the 1930s, when trucks and trailers were common, which probably explains why so little is left here. One can imagine the heartache of a miner when his life investment and dreams came to a sobering clash with reality. That tale was repeated hundreds of times in Death Valley, leaving evidence such as what we sift through.

People have always had crushing defeats—probably the true explorers and adventurers more frequently. Sometimes they discover or otherwise create something fantastic. In most cases, especially for Death Valley miners, they had to admit they were beaten and lick their wounds, deciding if this life of adventure should be continued or not. Without some small percentage of people like this, the human race would not have ventured from the African villages where our species originated. If we were all insatiably adventurous, though, we surely would not have created stable civilizations and cultures. I guess the ratio of adventurers to stable homebodies is about what it should be. I seem to be a mongrel blend of the two.

Today, the Desert Hound Mine is the end of our walk. There is plenty of time to poke around and rest. Chris and Brad are willing to explore a few feet into the mine around rotted timbers that appear way too sketchy for the rest of us, especially considering there is a shaft of indeterminate depth to fall into. There are no other hikers to share the site with, so we fan out to claim flat spots around the mine to spread our pads and sleeping bags. Speaking of no other hikers, this is again a typical trip for us in that we don't see anyone else the whole time. Brad develops hikes to places where that is usually the case. He also picked a hike this time that wasn't too ambitious in daily mileage or obstacles to climb up or around. Nobody is complaining that it is too easy. Maybe we've become a bunch of slackers?

The weather remains temperate, the stars are beautiful, and the night is long. Without chairs or lights, it is easy to default to begin laying in the sleeping bag at an earlier time than one would usually go to bed. This hilltop is not as soft as the stream bed, and a pad that is 3/4" thick feels luxurious at first, but by about 4:00 a.m. your hip bones are getting bruised. The 14" thick mattress at home is too heavy to put on the pack, so I make do with this thinner pad.

The next day we retrace our steps for a half mile, hoping again to locate the north branch of the Desert Hound Trail. To nobody's surprise (except Brad and me), we find the connection. This is a much better-marked trail, and we don't have to guess that we are going in the correct direction. Before descending this high area, we come to a saddle at about 4,300' elevation. The views are spectacular all around us. We have a snack, and we all lie down on the rocks for a nap in the sun.

The beautiful view did not prevent us from napping.

From here it is mostly downhill, and in another mile or so the trail becomes one with the area's drainage. The trail is erased in this stream bed, but it doesn't matter now. Despite the fact that there are narrow places and no marked trail, things are a lot more certain. The map from Digonnet shows that we just follow the drainage down to Virgin Spring Canyon, and then south, down that canyon. As we have found out several times previously, following drainage downhill is nearly always problem-free, because mountain streams don't branch as they are heading down; they just converge. Finding a path upstream is where problems occur, because there are an increasing number of choices and the one true path is rarely obvious. A mile or two further and we are down to about 2,500' elevation, where the Rock House ruins are. (This small structure of piled rocks was not named after me). We stop for the night here, after another relatively less challenging day, especially since it has been downhill. We are again pleased about how easy it is to find a fairly soft place to unroll a pad and bag when camping in a stream bed.

In the morning, we pack up and just head down the wide stream bed, only having to descend about 1,300 feet and walk about four miles. The first interesting thing to happen is that we find a Mylar birthday balloon, still partially inflated, stuck on a plant by its dangling ribbon. How far has this balloon travelled? Maybe 50, 100, or 150 miles? Being in a festive and environmentally conscious spirit, we attach it to my backpack.

We soon get a tremendous scare as two fighter jets come screaming down this canyon that is less than half a mile wide, barely above us, navigating the bends with eerie precision. The first thing we think is that if these weren't friendly aircraft, we'd be dead before we could finish the sentence, "What the—!" The second is that if they miscalculate any of their turns, there will be what is professionally referred to as an aluminum shower. The third thing we wonder is if they should be practicing maneuvers in the canyon of a national park. The Naval Air Weapons Station China Lake shares the southwestern boundary of DVNP, and the National Training Center at Fort Irwin shares the southern border, so it is probably quite a temptation to zoom into the virtually vacant national park and play in the canyons.

It is only midmorning when we get to the cars, so we have time for one more experience. We drive back towards Furnace Creek, where there is a two-mile-long graded dirt road up an alluvial fan to Mosaic Canyon. We park the

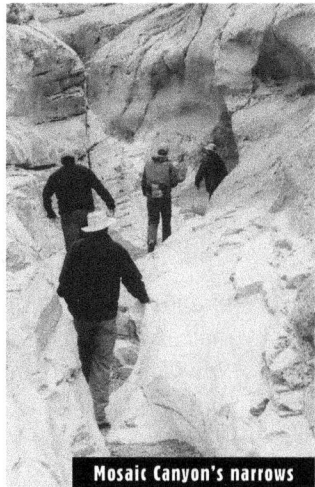

**Mosaic Canyon's narrows**

cars in the big lot and take a hike. The path soon enters a narrow formed by beautiful dolomite that has been stream-washed smooth. Some people might find it too hard to clamber through these boulders, but kids and childlike adults have a blast here. The canyon then opens to a sandy wash that has interesting side washes, one of which we enter to climb up on a pile of enormous boulders to have lunch. It is beautiful and liberating not to have our heavy packs.

There is a ridge to walk along that is probably unsafe and dumb to follow, so only Brad and I do so. When I go back down to the wash, John and I link arms in a moment of silly exuberance and skip for a while like the companions in the Wizard of Oz on the yellow brick road. We are pretty good at it! This is something I haven't done before or since and have no logical explanation for. It would have been inconceivable with any adult male other than John, and neither of us uses psychotic drugs. BJ has it on video, for better or worse.

## Hiking Lessons

1.  *If you only have one day for a hike, go up Mosaic Canyon. It's easy enough to access, and you'll see some of the best of DVNP without most of the challenges.*

2.  *There are not many others out there who can deal with the particularities of hiking with us. Way to go, Chris.*

3.  *These various versions of DVNP hikes with my friends continue to be therapeutic.*

## Life Lessons

1.  *Was this hike in Virgin Spring Canyon a predictor of my moving later this year to Nevada to manage the Virgin Valley Water District along the Virgin River? Normally I wouldn't use the word virgin, and soon it is to become something I write and say several times a day. That coincidence is beyond odd, I think.*

2.  *If you aren't spontaneous and silly sometimes, you don't have any memories like John and me skipping down the Mosaic Canyon wash. It will never leave my brain. Then again, maybe you don't want to have any memories like that.*

# 2011

# A Pretty Good Year, Even Without DVNP

## With Family & Friends

Late in 2010, Voni and I moved to Mesquite, Nevada, and it has seemed like a grand adventure. Our new house is twice as big and beautiful and was purchased at a much lower price than the one in San Jose. My wife and I, who were previously unknown outside our cul-de-sac, are now on this little town's celebrity list because of my new position as general manager of the Virgin Valley Water District. We are in a desert location, a short drive from beautiful national parks less enormous but as magnificent as Death Valley.

DVNP is an annual itch—my wife would call it an obsession—but I can't take vacation time in my first six months on this job, so I have to pass on a DVNP adventure. Death Valley is only 200 miles from here, but a weekend isn't long enough to be part of that adventure in the winter of 2011.

I work hard to make up for it. An almost unspoiled section of the Virgin Mountains, which defines the south border of our valley, is being considered as a national preserve called Gold Butte. There are spectacular petroglyphs in the sandstone formations, introduced to me by the wonderful newspaper editor David Bly. I get to take Voni there as well, on the passably smooth dirt road.

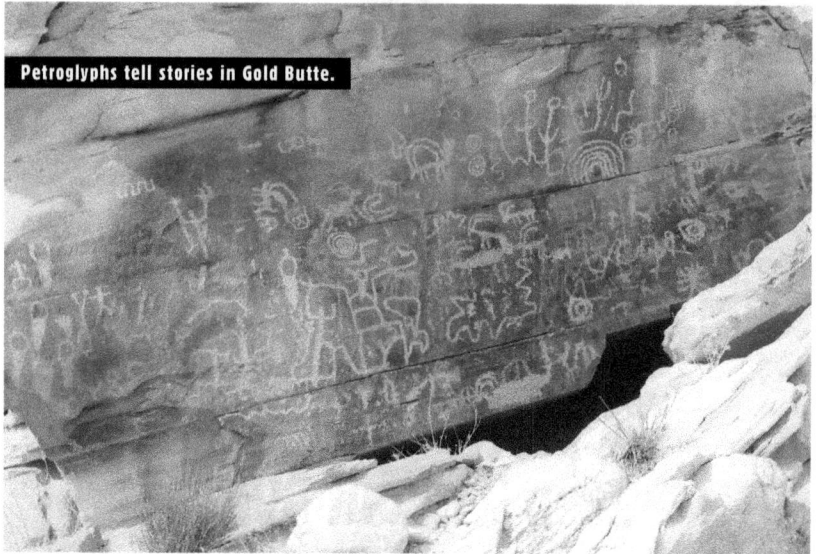

Petroglyphs tell stories in Gold Butte.

Zion National Park is only ninety minutes away from home. On a weekend, Voni and I take my father and stepmother to Zion, and we walk up The Narrows, a scenic, shady path along the Virgin River. On a later weekend, a couple that had been our neighbors in San Jose come to visit, and we go back to Zion to climb Angels Landing, an unforgettable hike with a world-class view from the top. Being able to take day trips to Zion from home is an incredible opportunity.

In the summer, I'm able to get away for a couple of days to go to Lundy Lake and meet with my oldest friend, Duane. Lundy is in the eastern Sierra Nevada Mountains, just west of Mono Lake. It is, like DVNP, as much home to me as anywhere. Lundy has healed my heart when it was broken.

Late in the summer, I'm able to take Voni to Yosemite National Park, a place so special that it is nearly perpetually overcrowded. The waterfalls and granite monoliths have to be experienced, though. On the way back, we drive through Death Valley, but the summer is not a gracious time to be visiting there. We don't spend more than ten minutes outside the van.

In late autumn, I get to take Voni and her friend to a time-share near Yellowstone National Park. There is more geothermal activity in Yellowstone than anywhere else in the world. Geysers are special. In Yellowstone, one can also see elk, wolves, and bears. As far as scenery goes, though, it doesn't hold a candle to any of the other places we see this year or to DVNP.

This is a book about Death Valley and my hiking friends, but 2011 turns out to be an exceptionally good year for visiting places of natural beauty. This year just doesn't include the regular guys and has only a cameo appearance of DVNP.

## Hiking Lessons

1.  *This year we hiked on paved trails in Zion, Yosemite, and Yellowstone National Parks. They don't require boots or walking shoes. Non-out-doorsy people get to experience natural beauty. That is healthy for them and society.*

2.  *By its nature, Death Valley will remain the best spot for solitude and the type of hiking adventures that my troop usually takes.*

## Life Lessons

1.  *Death Valley is only one of many national parks. Judging by the crowds we saw everywhere else, DVNP isn't so easily embraced, and that makes it better for our hiking foursome, which seeks solitude. It is good, though, that people are finding the commune with nature that they need in many other places. Hooray for the National Park System!*

2.  *While the magic lasts in Mesquite, it's grand to be there.*

# Surprise Canyon & Panamint City

*Deluxe One-Star Accommodations*

ife is still good in Mesquite, Nevada, and our team is ready for another DVNP adventure. Every year so far, we have explored somewhere that Michel Digonnet describes in *Hiking Death Valley*. It seems odd that this year Brad has a route planned that we can't find in our books. Instead, Brad sends us a two-sided flyer from the Bureau of Land Management (BLM) Ridgecrest Field Office. After a couple of years of long loops up and down canyons hoping to find a car we left two days ago, this year's adventure seems relatively tame.

The destination is Panamint City, on the west side of the Panamint Mountains in Surprise Canyon. According to Digonnet, it was originally the home to 1,000 silver miners. It boomed in the late 1800s, was wiped out by two summer storms in 1887 that took almost 200 lives, then was levelled again twenty-five years later by another summer flood. That crop of miners finally gave up.

In the early 1980s, Panamint City again had a relatively large and more modern mining operation, with another gravel access road laid over the rocky falls in narrow Surprise Canyon. In 1984, another flash flood scoured the canyon (surprise!) and roadway down to bedrock. This latest generation of miners gave up like those before. That was a good decision for them, as there have been a couple more flash floods since then, to boot. Maybe there is a lesson here about building stuff in narrow desert canyons, especially in Death Valley?

Digonnet describes how to access Panamint City from the eastern side of the range via an interesting but arduous hike over the mountain. It has taken me a while to realize why he speaks only of that route, considering that Panamint City is so historically significant, and Michel certainly knows that most of his readers are less capable than he. The reason must be that the access point from the west is in BLM lands. The border of DVNP is several miles east, up Surprise Canyon, and Panamint City is about a mile further. So, officially our hike from the west doesn't start in DVNP. The fact that much of the wreckage left in Panamint City is relatively new, in Death Valley terms, may diminish the rustic feel of the place, but Brad thinks that it will still be intriguing to see what is left. It turns out that he is right.

John, Johnny, and I meet in the morning at a place called Ballarat, at the southwest corner of the Panamint Mountains. Brad has to work today and will arrive later this evening. That Ballarat even has a name is amazing, because it consists of one ramshackle not-quite-a-store with an attached residence, both being somewhat the worse for wear. Historically, though, according to John Soennichsen in his book *Live from Death Valley: Dispatches from America's Low Point*, Ballarat was once a thriving place and "the favorite watering hole in the Panamint Valley." These days you can purchase interesting things in the tiny store, such as highly unusual meats not available anywhere else, but you won't find most of the sundries that are stocked in conventional stores. We claim something like a campsite nearby since Brad asked us to meet at Ballarat. Meanwhile, we have several hours to kill. There is nothing that captures our interest in the immediate, rather bleak area, so we drive north a few miles on the dirt road and then take that road up an alluvial fan to the base of Surprise Canyon.

We park at the road's end, where the Chris Wicht Camp is supposed to be. We can tell that this used to be a fine, shady, and spacious campground in a canyon with large trees. Soennichsen tells us that Chris Wicht was the bartender at the Ballarat Saloon from 1908 to nearly 1920, and Wicht rode his horse daily to and from this quiet retreat to his rowdy bar. There is water here, coming down from high-flow springs up Surprise Canyon, so the trees used to be magnificent. Unfortunately, all that remains are blackened trunks and charred stone building foundations. The fire that wiped out this resort was only a year or two ago. Before then, it would have been a much better place to camp than our current default spot in the desert pan. We can see why Wicht chose to live here.

A decent stream runs down the north side of this canyon opening, and in it is a large piece of yellow-painted steel equipment. It turns out that this is part of a mucker, used to clear debris out of a mine. We will see the other half about a mile up the canyon. A wall of flood water broke and pushed this heavy equipment for miles down the canyon. It is more evidence that flash floods in Surprise Canyon are not to be trifled with.

There is a clear trail that leads up the canyon. We shrug on light packs and surrender to its call. Apparently this has become, at least in DVNP terms, a rather popular path. That is understandable, since the steep canyon walls and continuously running water in the narrow floor make for a shady, cool, and green walk, conditions inconceivable for most of this national park. Being in BLM land, a few decades ago extreme four-wheel-drive vehicles winched and climbed up this path to Panamint City. The practice was ended in 2001 due to environmental concerns, so now it is serene here and most of the vehicular damage has been erased by subsequent flash floods. We're glad for the current conditions. This accessible hike, it turns out, is doable for almost anyone with decent fitness, some perseverance, and a sense of adventure.

Well, mostly. The canyon narrows over the next mile until the stream occupies the entire floor and forms some falls. Wow, waterfalls flowing with water—a really strange condition near DVNP. They aren't dramatic falls—more like a hundred feet of rugged, irregular stair-stepped polished limestone with water running around and over it. Johnny has shorter legs and is a bit less agile, but he still gets up with just a little coaxing and moist boots. Oh, and no complaints. Johnny never complains.

The canyon stays under 100 feet wide, so it is understandable that the trail easily becomes clear again after the falls, with so little space to wander. We follow it for a couple more miles until we come to an area of extensive vegetation where Brewery Spring feeds this watery miracle. This is a good place to relax and enjoy lunch. The canyon has colorful steep walls, we have a choice of shade or sunshine, and water is nearby. Life is peaceful and good here.

We decide that this is far enough for today because we want to leave some new experiences for tomorrow when we hike with Brad the rest of the way to Panamint City. Today's hike back down is uneventful, with nobody getting very wet or falling. With heavy packs tomorrow it will be more challenging, but we are confident that we will be successful.

People don't come from around the world to camp in the scenic beauty at Ballarat. Regardless, we have our own good company, and the panoramic view to the west is pretty fair. If it were summer this would be hellish, but tonight in January the weather is balmy. We create our gourmet dinners and wait for BJ. After dark, a car comes up the dirt road—there isn't a lot of traffic here. It is Brad, who rolls down the window, acts confused, and asks if we know the way to Ridgecrest. Ha ha.

In the morning, we do our usual routine to break camp and drive the few miles back to the former Chris Wicht Camp. We load up our packs, which are a few pounds lighter than usual because we don't bother carrying more than a half gallon of water in each. It is feeling more normal now, the four of us with everything on our backs and a new destination ahead. The falls are more challenging with full loads, but we don't have to shed the packs to get up. Our walking sticks prevent any human falls in the water falls. We stop again at Brewery Spring, inspired by yesterday's stop here.

It seems like a long way to the smokestack of the foundry built for the 1980s mining operation. OK, maybe it's only four or five miles to here, at the western margin of Panamint City. What we weren't thinking about, for some reason, is that the climb has been steady. The start of the hike was at about 3,000' to 4,000' elevation, and Panamint City is spread around at about 6,300' elevation. We keep marching along, seeing that the place is quite vast, dispersed in this high pocket valley about a mile wide and long and defined by steep mountains thousands of feet higher.

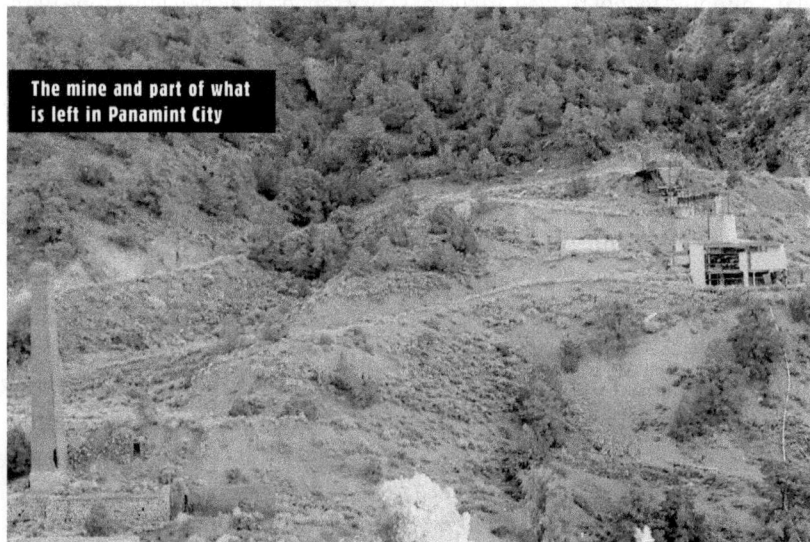

The mine and part of what is left in Panamint City

Most of the remaining buildings in this ghost town are 1980s vintage, cheap but still somehow classic, because they are simple rough wood on rock foundation. The valley floor doesn't have structures. That makes sense, as a storm over this valley would have all of the rain focused to the floor in short order, washing away anything wooden; gaining volume, it would soon scour away foundations, vehicles, and boulders in a gathering flash flood. A thoughtful geologist who wasn't spending all of their energy on mapping silver deposits might have predicted flash floods and warned the investors and occupants not to build on the valley floor. History tells us that lesson wasn't learned, even after repeated disasters. Some people are dangerously stubborn, perhaps even by my standards. Now, in retrospect, the conditions for a flash flood appear perfectly formed, even to an under-qualified not-really-geologist.

There are numerous buildings to poke in, and we are eventually drawn to a cabin on a pine-shaded slope. It has a porch with a long wood bench, and the setting is idyllic. The cabin's size is about 600 square feet, and all of the windows and doors are intact. It is too tempting not to call this mansion our home for the night.

We like the outside of the cabin as much as the inside. That says a lot because the interior has a counter and a sink. We reason that a sink must have had a water supply at some time, even though it is dry now. We have time and energy, so we decide to find out where the water came from so that we can replenish our bottles. We trace a white PVC pipe behind the cabin, follow it up a slope, and find, in a few hundred feet, the end of the pipe in a pool at a spring. Well, shucks, this setup is only thirty years old, so let's try to fix it. We tape together some breaks in the pipe and muck out the pool. The spring flows at about ten gallons per minute, so it flushes out fairly quickly. My work experience is in water and wastewater treatment, plus I've built a few irrigation systems, so this feels like a familiar task in a beautiful setting with good friends. We find a few tools and spare parts to help the cause. It's really fun, in a strange way. But, then, every year we have fun doing what many people would call strange.

Back at the cabin, the water flows from the faucet with a decent pressure, although it initially comes out dark and disgusting. We congratulate ourselves on our engineering genius, getting flowing water into an abandoned cabin at about 6,400' elevation. The place has definitely earned one star in the AAA rating system.

It is getting cooler but there is still some daylight, so we venture out to explore a bit more. We find a small cave, which is really just a massive flat-based boulder that is resting on some slightly less massive boulders against a hillside. We crawl inside and the ceiling-covering petroglyphs are stunning. The Native Americans painted here with orange, yellow, and white. There are animals of various depictions and shapes of horns interspersed with human shapes of different sizes and proportions. There is at least one archer among them. We are amazed that none of the miners who lived here defaced this. It makes one hope that perhaps they actually had some sense of cultural value. My guess is that it's more likely that there was a persistent story that the cave was haunted, and legend attributed some awful fate to anyone bold and stupid enough to anger the spirits. Hey, why take a chance, right? Mining is risky enough as it is.

We return to the cabin and again marvel at our good fortune to respectfully borrow it for the night. There was, or perhaps still is, an owner to this abode. Imagine having a comfortable place in a serene, beautiful location with running water. The only problem is that it is really difficult to access, so maintaining the cabin or even just bringing supplies becomes a logistics nightmare. I suppose mules could work but no longer any motor vehicles. Once Surprise Canyon became washed out for the umpteenth time and even four-wheel drive vehicles were banned, you'd be screwed. I hope they have good memories and plenty of photos. At least the cabin is swept out now, and the water runs for a while.

All of us opt to sleep outside on the porch or near the house, as the sky is cloudless and there is no wind. What is remarkable is how cold tonight is compared to last night in Ballarat, 5,000 feet lower in elevation. The stars are spectacular, and it is worth it.

A cold night generally means a cold morning. I am able to jump around enough to warm up a little and take photos of my three friends huddled and grinning on the porch with their cups of hot tea. Photos are mostly about subject and setting. This one becomes a classic.

We eventually gather our things and regretfully say goodbye to this sweet location. We all have to get back to our regular worlds by this evening. As with most of our hikes, the return walk is less eventful. Being all downhill and with packs slightly lighter, it is also faster and easier. Gosh, we even have a real trail here for most of the time. I am glad that our hikes generally involve going uphill to explore the higher aspect of a canyon, so that the trip out doesn't become a bit of a death march. Leaving is bittersweet enough as it is.

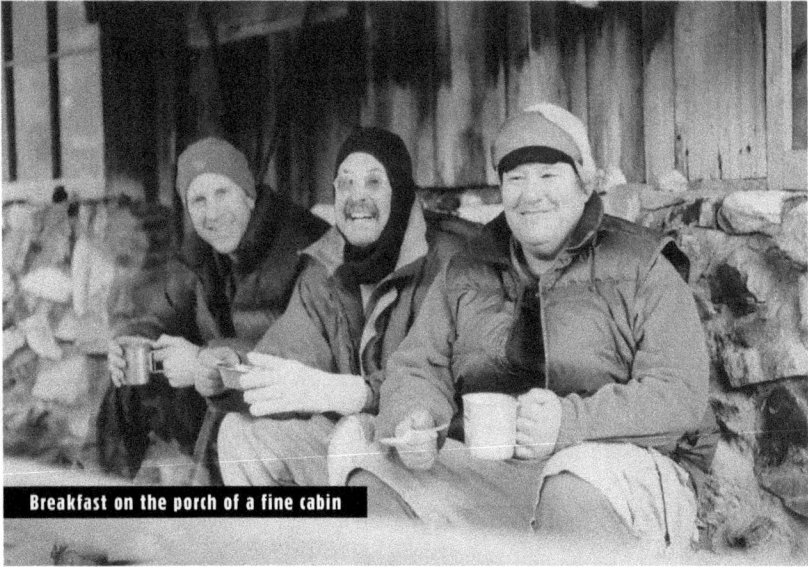

Breakfast on the porch of a fine cabin

We know the routine. Dump the pack into the car, rehydrate, switch out boots for sneakers, hug farewell, and promise to meet for another adventure a year from now.

## Hiking Lessons

1. *Again, walking sticks are a good thing. Even if you just carry them over a lot of easy trail, when it gets unstable, they make a big difference.*

## Life Lessons

1. *If you happen to be the family who owns a seemingly deserted cabin in Panamint City, thanks for letting us use it. We left it a little better than we found it.*

2. *Never deface Native American art or you might have a very angry spirit torment you.*

3. *Be aware of grades and the potential flow of water before you build. If you can find the history of the flooding pattern in an area, don't ignore it. The residents in Panamint City paid the price.*

4.  *I could and should have analyzed grades when I selected our house in Mesquite, Nevada, at the base of a hill. In the summer of 2012, the little dirt berm at the back of our property did not hold back the torrent of water from a night storm, and we woke in the morning to a completely flooded house. The psychological and financial damage are hard to express. Unlike most of the Panamint City miners, I should have had the wherewithal to recognize and avoid or prepare for that inevitable event.*

# TIMELESS

## Fun in a Place Called Death Valley

*Some Unusual Behavior*

When we have babies or grandchildren around, it is acceptable to be silly and laugh. If left alone, we crave a smile so much that we are willing to pay to have someone else make us laugh. Once out of college and in the usual business of life, though, most of us go forever without creating a fun and nonsensical scenario for ourselves. It's unprofessional or it could give us a rumor-feeding reputation. We might be ostracized or reported to some authorities as unstable or dangerous. It's risky.

In Death Valley, where nobody else is watching and just being there means we are committed to days of impractical behavior, we would do things beyond what we'd consider doing elsewhere. (Well, John might consider it, but most of us would not.)

Some of that stuff got photographically recorded.

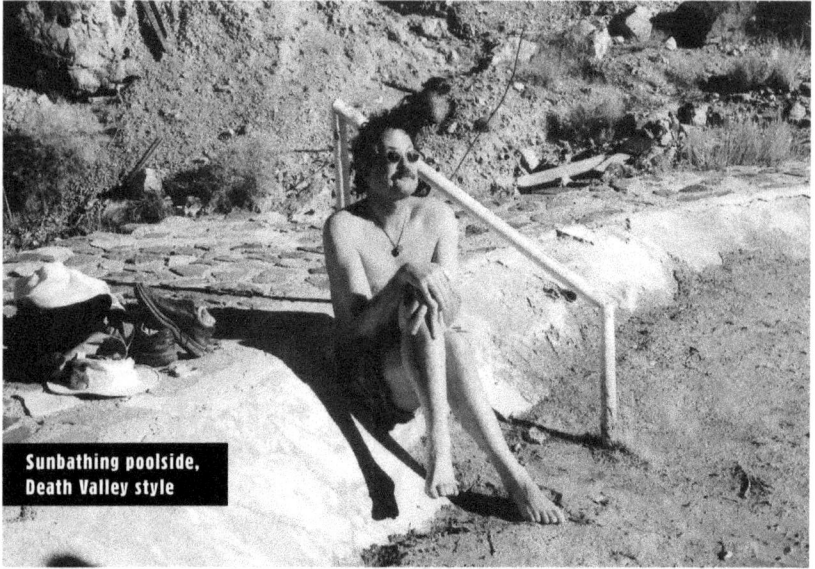

Sunbathing poolside, Death Valley style

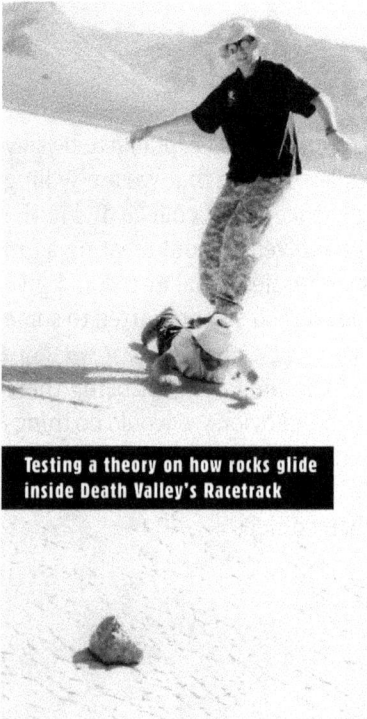

Testing a theory on how rocks glide inside Death Valley's Racetrack

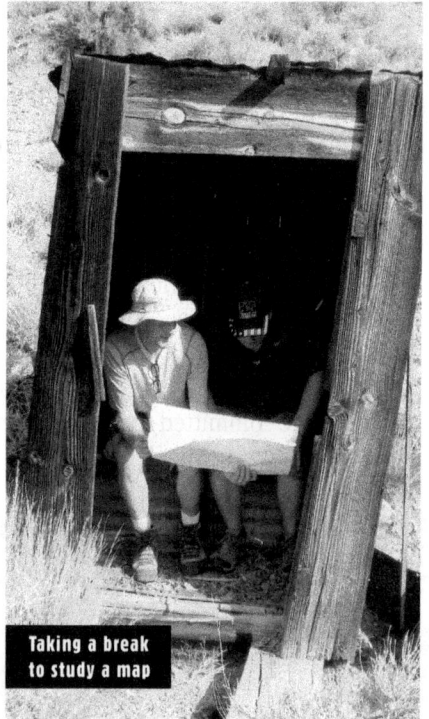

Taking a break to study a map

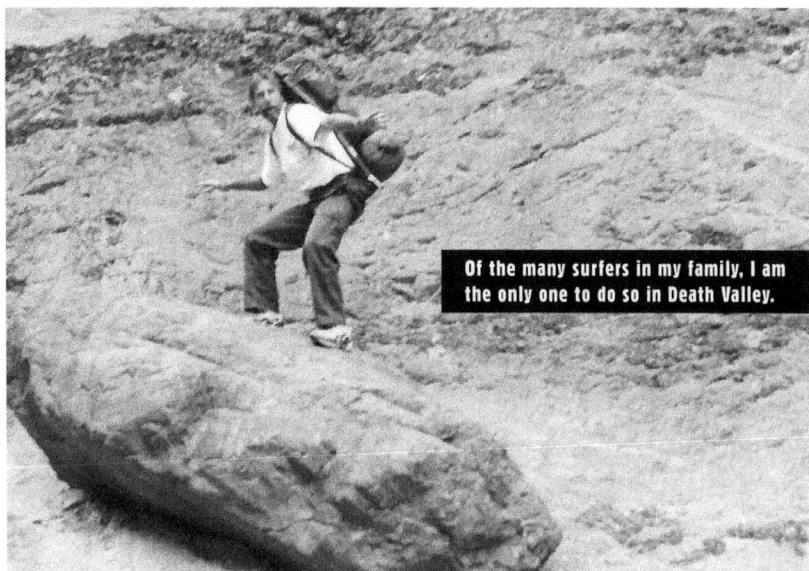

Of the many surfers in my family, I am the only one to do so in Death Valley.

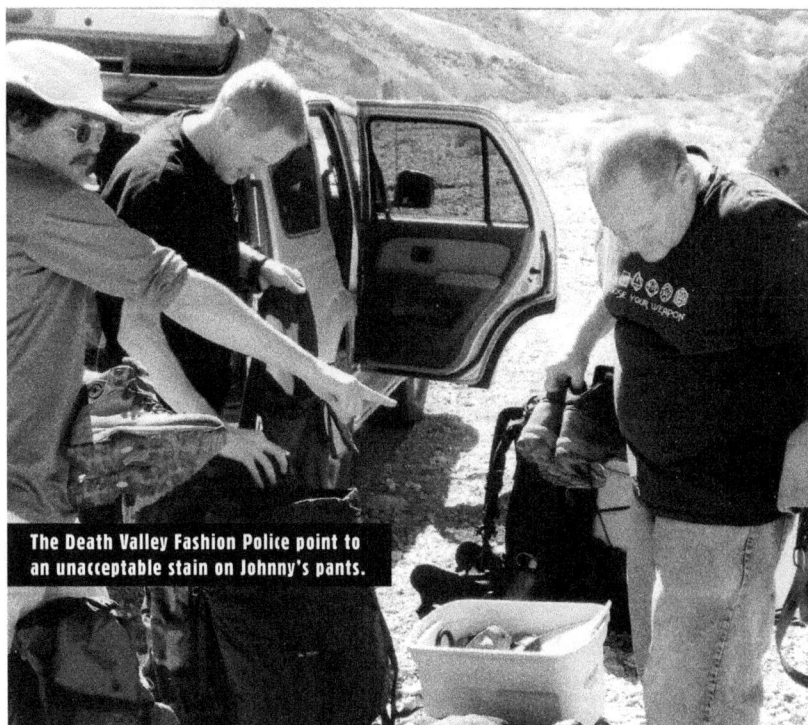

The Death Valley Fashion Police point to an unacceptable stain on Johnny's pants.

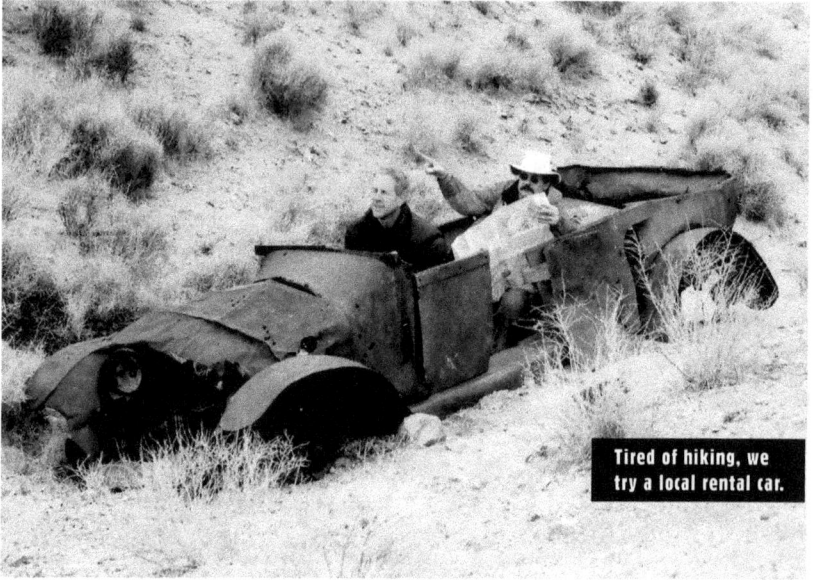

Tired of hiking, we try a local rental car.

Doogie "boldly goes where no man has gone before," which is first base with Johnny.

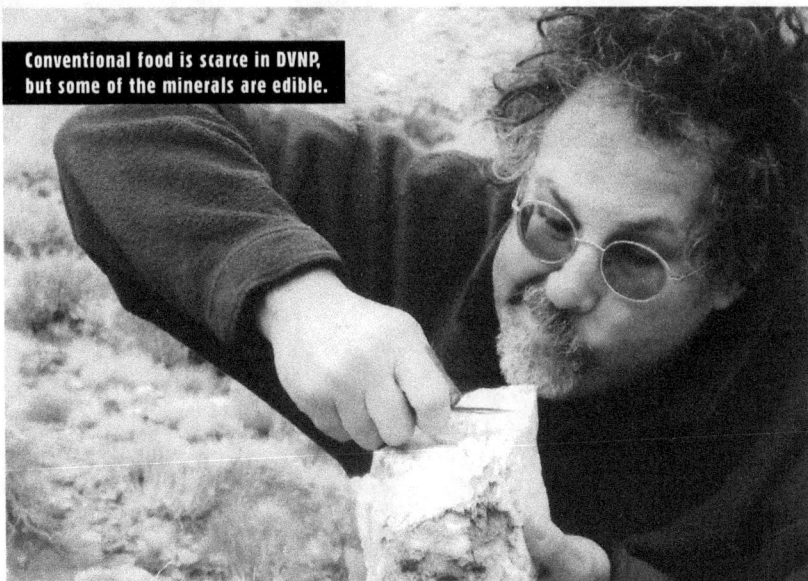

Conventional food is scarce in DVNP, but some of the minerals are edible.

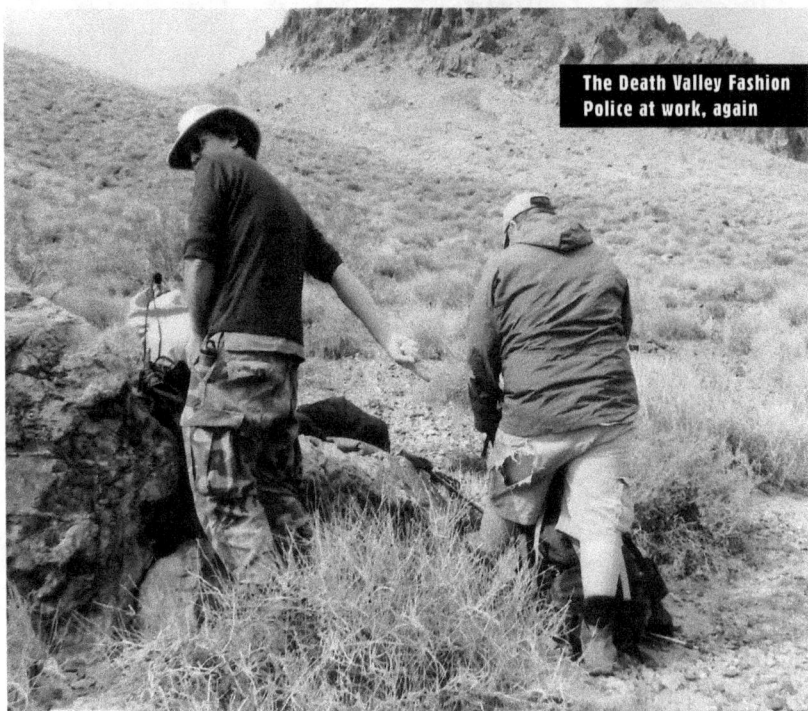

The Death Valley Fashion Police at work, again

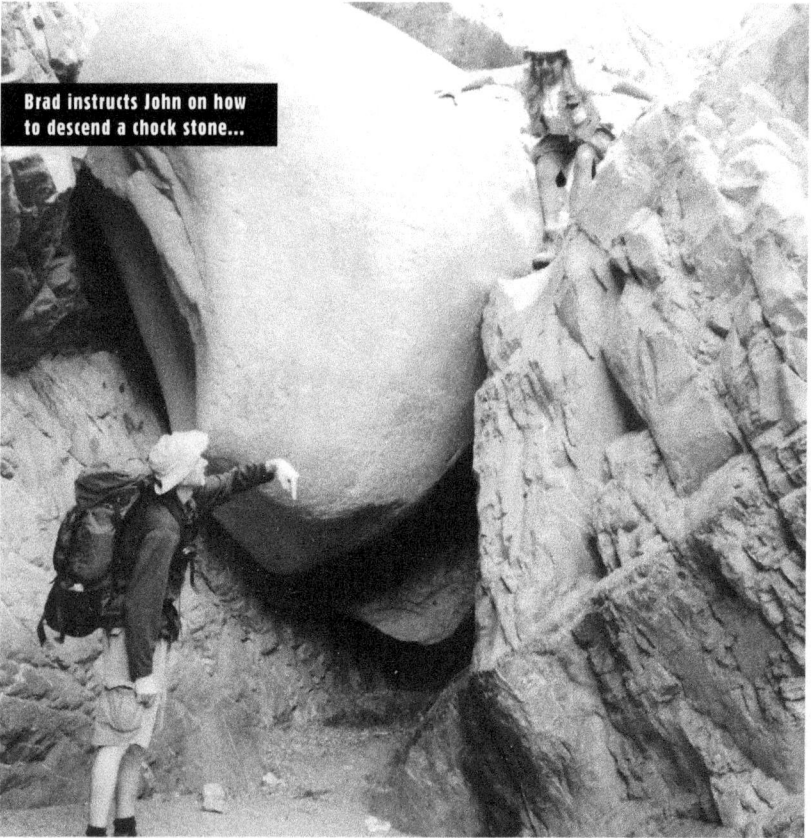

Brad instructs John on how to descend a chock stone...

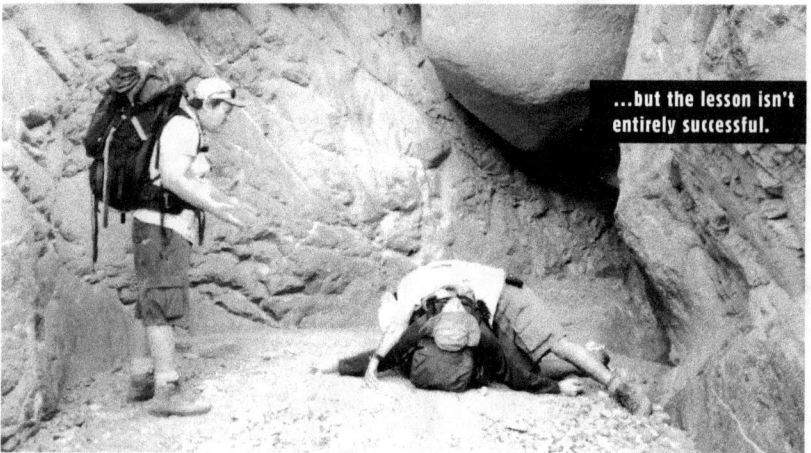

...but the lesson isn't entirely successful.

# 2013

# Slit Canyon, Echo Canyon, & Nevares Springs

*Cabin of Zombies*

It is warm mid-March and I have arrived alone and a day early to claim a campsite in a regular valley-floor campground called Texas Spring, near Furnace Creek. There are restrooms with running water and a picnic table at each site, but the ground surface is just dirt and there is no shade. I suppose this is fine for people with recreational vehicles or even tents, but for our type of camping it seems like a strange combination of civility and poor bedding conditions too close to other humans and their vehicles. In any case, I go for a hike in the afternoon for a couple of miles up from the campground to a spring, then return to sit on the bench and quietly play the guitar. As I go to sleep, I briefly wonder why I came here alone a day ahead of the other guys. Oh, now I remember why I have extra time this year. I'm unemployed because last month I was fired from the general manager position for the Virgin Valley Water District. Three of the five board members thought I was too progressive because of my efforts to determine the sustainable water supply for our desert basin, which is shared by three states. One of the board members even suggested that I might be an environmentalist, as if that is an insult rather than a credit for a water manager. Last summer our dream house flooded, and now I've been fired. I'm feeling incompetent and unsuccessful—and like a poor spouse. Maybe some time in DVNP will help mend me enough to move ahead.

The rest of the team arrives the next morning at Furnace Creek, where we meet to get our backcountry permit and have breakfast. Somehow, Johnny spills a full cup of coffee on his pants, and fortunately it is not hot enough to burn him. Once we know that he is OK, it is fun to frequently ask him how the brown stain got on the front of his pants. After the last year, almost anything is funny.

It is always great to see the guys again. Apparently, they don't mix much during the year either, so it is as much of a reunion for them as it is for me. In my observation, this type of bonding that does not require frequent reinforcement is not as common with the female of our species. They think it is weird. A lot of male behavior, like these DVNP hikes, seems peculiar to many women.

This year, BJ has ambitiously set up two hikes for us. The first will be an overnight adventure where we'll leave my Honda Element in one desolate canyon, then drive Brad's Toyota FJ many miles around to another improbable place. We will then find our way cross-country to the first car. The next day, we will hike up to Nevares Springs in a completely different area.

We set out for our first adventure. It requires that we drive on Highway 190 for 2.1 miles north, past Badwater Road, to a dirt road east into the Funeral Mountains on the east border of DVNP. We go about ten miles up the primitive road in Echo Canyon to almost 3,800' elevation, where the Inyo Mine and Camp are. We see no other people or vehicles. It seems bizarre to leave the Honda here near the end of a canyon. We all pile into Brad's Toyota and head back down this dirt road, east on Highway 190, and then up another dirt road for a few miles. We park at a place called Hole-in-the-Wall, at about 1,800' elevation. It's not really a hole as much as a 200-foot-wide gap in a sheer wall over 300 feet high and two miles long. On the south side is the wash we drove up, and on the other side of the wall is the alluvial fan for this part of the Funeral Mountains. It's all pretty weird and seems like a highly improbable geologic formation, and yet it exists.

We shoulder our packs and tromp through the gap and up the alluvial fan to a narrow canyon hidden over a mile to the north. There are several canyons that feed this fan, but only one, Slit Canyon, will get us toward our other well-hidden car. BJ shares his topo map with John and me, and we agree that if we steer left along the west wall of this hemmed-in fan, the correct canyon will present itself. As usual, Johnny admits that maps and he don't understand each other well, so he trusts us to determine the course.

The hiking isn't too difficult here, as this alluvial fan is more like a wide wash. The sunny weather is pleasant. In a little over a mile, it becomes apparent that there is a narrow canyon where we are headed, and soon after entering the canyon's opening, the walls become sheerer, closing into a steep, polished dolomite, twelve-foot fall. This would not be a significant barrier for a skilled rock climber, but for us, to varying degrees, it is somewhere between interesting and seemingly impossible. We decide that the packs will all have to be roped up. Brad climbs the falls without any drama, and I ascend somewhat less skillfully by a route that looks easier to me. John and Johnny attach our bags one at a time to a rope, which BJ and I pull up. These things are heavy.

Now for the tough part. Brad descends, and then he and John form a human climbing ladder for Johnny to get up the first five feet, standing on Brad's shoulders. I descend partway and lend a hand to help pull Johnny up. Frankly, it is pretty scary, as Johnny outweighs any of us. Brad grunts something about "he ain't heavy, he's my brother." The only saving grace is that if some of us fall, the landing surface is soft sand, albeit further away than any of us would volunteer to jump to—and we'd likely break each other's bones in the pileup. Johnny bravely does a rock-hugging crawl and, with pulls, pushes, and encouragement, he succeeds in bellying up to the top. It is one of those times when hyperventilation is appropriate for all of us—particularly Johnny, who sprawls in a safe place next to the packs.

Brad throws the walking sticks up to me and again expertly climbs the fall. John has corralled his courage and decided that he can climb this. He picks the direction that I took and slowly ascends. At the top of this route, you have to sidle sideways across a sheer drop while letting go of a handhold. John freezes and begins to shake with an "I'm going to die!" look in his eyes. I know that scary feeling, but there is no safe way for me to reach clear over to him. BJ and I manage to coax him to handholds and footholds that inch him over and then we pull him. He collapses next to Johnny.

Nice start! In short order, we encounter two more even taller falls in quick succession, but Digonnet has described a work-around that involves scrambling up a talus slope on the eastern side. A talus is just a jumbled mess of unconsolidated rock of various sizes and is generally not a favored surface to traverse. In this situation, there are some larger rocks that hold our weight as we clamber, so we don't have much trouble with the material shifting as we climb it.

In another thousand feet or so in these wonderful narrows, we come to the mother of all DVNP falls. It is fifty feet of sheer drop, all polished, shiny, smooth dolomite. Fortunately, again, Digonnet describes a work-around involving another talus slope. This one is not as stable or short, and we would not have selected this direction if the other option wasn't completely impossible. There is a lot of reliance on walking sticks as we slowly test each movement up over the hump and then down to the canyon floor above the fall. It has taken hours of time and work to get less than half a mile up this appropriately named Slit Canyon. We break for lunch and plop onto the sand of the marvelous narrows as we measure our success.

The narrows where we eat lunch are winding and only fifteen to thirty feet wide. It is special not just because of the beauty, but also because few people have climbed up or around those falls to get here. We are not only alone, but we may also be the first people to step in this wash in a long time.

As we continue, we encounter a wider section of the canyon, then another narrows for a few hundred feet, then a slightly wider section, and then a third narrows. More challenges await. In these last narrows, we have to rope up the packs to get past several additional nine- to twelve-foot falls. Fortunately, none of them cause our hearts to race or stop as much as the first falls did today. Maybe we are getting a little better at this?

When we get past the third narrows and set of falls, we have travelled less than four miles since leaving the car, but it is already late afternoon. The canyon opens up here, and the sandy riverbed is easy walking. Before we go much further, we decide that this place, with many sandy benches for sleeping (and out of the narrows where a flash flood would kill us), is perfect. We've ascended about 2,300 feet with our packs, up to around 4,100' elevation. It's high enough to make for a cooler night. Yeah, let's not walk further.

Johnny really is Brad's brother-in-law (so the "he ain't heavy" line was appropriate), but we do all feel like brothers. It is a satisfying mutual success that we experience now after going the length of Slit Canyon as a team. Since we are all fully unbroken, BJ's hiking path was great as a bonding exercise. Successfully meeting a challenge with the support of others I respect is a needed balm for my battered ego.

Sand makes for a perfect surface under a thin pad. When the temperature is in the 50s, a cheap sleeping bag like mine is also perfect if you wear most of your clothes to bed. That works for me, having inherited some of my father's depression-era frugality that says to keep using something if it is still mostly functional. A really superior bag like the other guys have would cost $300. On most of our trips, a lighter sleeping bag has worked out fine. A sketchy memory for the coldest nights and an irrational sense of adventure complete my reasoning for continuing to use this bag.

So, it's not too cold, partially because I'm inside my little two-man tent. Halfway through the night, we are awakened by fat raindrops and Johnny yelling, "Guys! Guys!" We spring into action and lean Johnny-in-a-bag up against a boulder so we can wrap him in waterproof plastic. Propped-up is how he wants to spend the night. Next, for some reason bordering on mindless chivalry and adventure, I surrender my tent to Doogie and BJ, and let them wrap me and my sleeping bag in a plastic sheet.

The rain never gets through the wrappers around Johnny and me, although the patter does get a bit loud at times. For Brad and John, the rest of the night is perhaps even less comfortable. It turns out that the tent I so gallantly let them use is not waterproof and barely even water-resistant. They get to spend the rest of their night trying to stay dry in a defective enclosure.

In the morning, we awake to a relatively dry site. The other guys have their usual instant oatmeal with red pepper flakes. Don't knock it until you've tried it—this is now my go-to way of eating oatmeal. As of this morning, though, I'm still the man who eats handfuls of dry granola for breakfast, avoiding the need for dawn camp cooking. They boil more water and have tea in their cereal cups, to help clean out the residual oatmeal film. I've tried oatmeal-infused tea just to say that I've done it, but it is not a habit that I will embrace for my usual morning beverage. Some say that a used tea bag is also a therapeutic balm for facial skin care, but we've never taken our tea bag use to that degree. We have to keep our rugged male personas up, after all.

We stuff our packs, erase the meager evidence of our camp, and continue our hike up the canyon. It doesn't take long for the canyon to broaden and flatten further. In a mile or so, it rolls up to a ridge at about 4,800' elevation. There is a fierce, cold wind up here as we struggle to figure out how Digonnet is telling us to go cross country to find Echo Canyon. We can see where we probably need to cross over a broad saddle to the north at the same elevation, and Echo Canyon should be beyond it. Theoretically, we could take a contour along the side of this mountain without losing any elevation, and it would be the shortest distance to that saddle. I really want to do this, but the slope is uneven and a mile or more of walking on that is inviting disaster. We talk about the options but decide to take Digonnet's advice. We go east for half a mile to drop 250 feet lower into a wash and then walk north up the wash for a mile to get to that saddle. It works, and nobody gets hurt. So, shorter isn't always better.

From here, it should be only about a mile to Inyo Camp, but it is many hundreds of feet lower in a canyon that we can't see into. With a compass and some faith, we walk north down a fair slope into an unseen place that we think will hold a car that will get us out. I act more confident than recent events in my life would justify and march ahead with the hope that I won't lead my friends into some perilous condition.

If you are going to park a car in a place where you want to be able to see it from a long way away, make the car bright orange. We sight the Element half a mile away, and our spirits are high. Here we are in the midst of a large, abandoned gold-mining operation and there is a lot to see. We don't poke around for long, though. Today's challenges aren't quite complete.

A Honda Element has the ridiculously low maximum payload of 650 pounds. With four grown men, their heavy packs, and some other supplies, we are now pushing 1,000 pounds. My wife brings a lot of stuff on our road trips and we may also convey nearly that weight, but she and I never drive on unmaintained dirt roads. Downhill, cautiously, gravity works in our favor and not much grinds. Highway 190 is also fine. The gravel road up to Hole-in-the-Wall, however, is not fine. By the psychic will of four, a lot of throttle, a fair amount of grinding the undercarriage, and some luck, we get up the dirt road/gravel wash to Brad's more legitimate SUV.

I'm not sure why, but rather than camp here in a perfectly acceptable spot, we all drive back to the less-than-spectacular commercial campground that I had slept in a couple of days ago. Having toilets and showers are tonight's exchanges for a serene and beautiful location in higher country. Tomorrow we will remedy that, after a night on the dirt here.

In the morning we find it easy to rise, partly because it is not cold. It is also easier to cook and enjoy your oatmeal on a picnic bench. Using a flush toilet and brushing your teeth at a sink is surprisingly convenient. Throwing your bag into a car is also easier. There are some advantages to a developed campground that we must grudgingly admit to.

We drive our clean and properly toileted selves north a few miles past Furnace Creek Ranch on Highway 190 and park at the base of another large alluvial fan that spills down from the Funeral Mountains. There is a gulch in the hills to the east that Digonnet says will lead us toward Nevares Peak at 2,859' elevation. We don't think we'll get that far, but it is a goal. At least at the base of the mountain, where this alluvial fan originates, there is a spring and a cabin, both also named Nevares.

Oh, another alluvial fan—our favorite. At least we are all smart enough to have boots and walking sticks. Digonnet describes a route that is somewhat less arduous than trying to walk straight up the fan. We go east up a large wash for 2.5 miles, then south across the alluvial fan for 0.9 miles, where he says it is smoother. We know that trudging up gravel washes is not great, but it is better than the endless gullies that compose any Death Valley alluvial fan. We will start at minus 200' elevation, climb the wash to 1,130' elevation, and then find the cabin at about 850' elevation. I predict that we won't need to climb Nevares Peak for additional exercise today. It isn't the mileage as much as the terrain, packs, and climb that will take their toll.

Well, we come here for the challenge. We quickly get another lesson. DVNP near sea level in mid-March is very nice shirtsleeve weather, but it is getting hot for the work that we are doing and there is no hint of shade. It's not unbearably warm; it's just that we have been rather spoiled in our previous visits by not having to deal with anything resembling heat. This is our first DVNP hike that begins near or below sea level.

After what feels like more than two and a half miles, we climb out of the gully and are able to sight the trees to the south that mark Nevares Springs. We find an amazingly legitimate trail across here, with a surface packed hard enough for easy walking—especially since it is slightly downhill. I'm like a horse who smells water at the end of a day, and I run the last few hundred yards to the springs.

We strip down and are able to get wet in a few inches of clear water, refreshing ourselves. Nevares Peak looms over us about another nine miles away, and we agree unanimously that we really don't need to climb it. Being at the foot of a mountain is sometimes a suitable substitute for standing on top of it. From where we stand, it is certainly a lot easier.

On our walk to find nearby Nevares Cabin, we see evidence of how this place was cared for in the past. Digonnet says that Adolphus Nevares made Death Valley his home for fifty-two years, most of them in this homestead. He created a fruit orchard and vegetable garden watered from the springs. Next to what was a nice cabin is a root cellar; a large tamarisk tree forms a shaded yard on the other side of the cabin. We can understand how someone who doesn't need much company could find the solitude, combined with a panoramic view of Death Valley to the west and Nevares Peak to the east, idyllic.

It turns out that there is a dirt road straight up to nearly this location, but

What is left of Nevares's garden and cabin

it is rarely used and closed to the public. That means that very few people get here, which is apparent when we look into the cabin. It has been neglected but at least not vandalized, which is the fate of most abandoned buildings that miscreants don't have to work hard to access. Nevares's cabin will be our home tonight and he conveniently left behind a broom and some other household tools, so we set to sweeping and cleaning the place.

The "yard" under the tamarisk is a deep bed of fine needles, perfect for lounging and napping in the shade. We succumb to the temptation after our shared lunch of eclectic vittles. Yawn, who needs to climb a mountain today? Not us.

The rest of the afternoon passes pleasantly, with us reading and chatting. It is tempting to spend the night on this bed of needles, but we decide against it. This organic mat is several inches thick and with some deeper investigation we see that it is the home of many crawling things that might also investigate us in the night. DVNP camps don't usually have the consideration of what vermin might visit you, and we decide we don't need that in our bedding equation.

We filter spring water to fill all of our bottles—another pleasant luxury at this location. We study the topographic map and confirm that there is no freakin' way that we are climbing Nevares Peak today or tomorrow. Maybe we'll tackle that sometime in the future if we become younger. I can accept that neither will likely happen.

The cabin has a table and chairs—additional luxuries we almost never have. After our usual dinner of rehydrated food, we are content but so rested and comfortable that we don't need to sleep yet. I have a new digital camera and my headlamp has the option of a red light. We are inspired, and with John's candle and the red light we set about taking head shots in the window openings that make us look like zombies. It is fun to be alive—free to be acting like children without any judgement regarding the silliness of the activity, devoid of any practical justification.

**Friends can be zombies as well.**

You can bet that Nevares never had a similar evening of entertainment in his cabin. There is plenty of room for all four of us to lay out bedding, and we sleep comfortably. This is so much better than a campground on the valley floor surrounded by motor vehicles. I doubt that we'll do that again. Well, maybe we will when we're even older and can't hike up alluvial fans with heavy packs.

In the morning, we rise early enough to see the sun light up the Panamint Range across Death Valley to the west. We have to drive home today, but we know that the hike down won't be as arduous as yesterday's climb. The panoramic view of the valley and mountains is a lot easier to appreciate this morning with a less difficult walk and cooler morning air. It is almost as if we float down the wash—which in a sense we do, because it is just steep enough for our steps to get extended another inch with each descending placement in the loose gravel.

This has turned out to be another great trip, even if it did start out rather depressing for me. We have collected some fine panoramic photos, nice pictures of Nevares Cabin, and numerous rather weird shots of crooked crimson-hued disembodied heads propped in rustic window frames.

## Hiking Lessons

1.  *Tough is OK, if it doesn't break someone. Challenges make for vivid memories.*

2.  *If you study a map thoroughly and it looks like you know where you are going, then you probably do.*

3.  *Sometimes less is more. Trying to hike to Nevares Peak would have*

been too much for this team unless we had another full day and exceptional fitness.

4.    Although it is better for most folks, this group is not yet ready to embrace the RV campground thing.

## Life Lessons

1.    Why did it take me so long to go from film to a digital camera with a zoom lens? It has made creative photos so much easier.

2.    Some guys, like Mr. Nevares, make a life that they treasure even though it is mostly spent in isolation with no material riches. We are torn between being confounded with the justification for such a choice and envious of his simple lifestyle. There are moments, though, when many of us would like to walk away from whatever is torturing us and have no worries greater than keeping some of the spring water diverted into our gardens.

3.    I don't know where in the country my next job will be, but I feel more confident now about dedicating myself to finding it with minimal crisis to my wife. It is possible that I will never be able to see these guys and visit DVNP again, but it has been a good run.

The trail to Nevares Cabin has some views.

# 2014

# South Fork of Trail Canyon

*A Family Lived Here*

In October of 2013, I was hired in Scottsdale, Arizona. That is just weird, because the building where I work now is the very same one that Voni worked in when we met eighteen years ago, when she was the water conservation specialist for Scottsdale. For the sake of continuing the DVNP adventures, I have to travel an additional 200 miles each way, but it is worth it.

We hikers meet at Furnace Creek at 8:00 a.m. for our usual hearty breakfast and last use of a modern bathroom. This trip begins on January 31, and perhaps we hadn't fully thought through how the dead of winter and our destination at 4,400' elevation in the Panamint Mountains might make for cool nights. Again, the Panamint Mountains are the range that runs north-south in the southwest part of DVNP and seem to have no limit to their hidden wonders. Trail Canyon is about in the middle of this range, on the east side. It is accessed by a dirt road that is listed as requiring four-wheel-drive high-clearance vehicles.

Our goal is to go to the Morning Glory Mine camp and spring in the south fork of Trail Canyon via this primitive road that goes up the length of the canyon. With BJ driving a Toyota 4Runner and John and me in the Honda Element, we figure that we will at least make it partway up the road through the alluvium to the canyon and then hike the rest of the way. That turns out to be a fair assessment of how the trip starts. After grounding and bounding over some of the larger rocks in the wash, the Element, with front-wheel drive and road tires, eventually loses traction completely in the gravelly climb several miles up from the floor of Death Valley. A valiant effort by the Element. John and I pile into the 4Runner and get another quarter mile or so further before it encounters the same fate. Well, that was fun—and just mildly destructive to our vehicles. At least we are now only four or five miles from our destination and have gained 2,000 to 3,000 feet in elevation. We have seen nobody else and won't for this whole experience.

I've noted before how hiking up a gravel wash with a heavy pack is arduous, right? What is listed as a primitive road hardly seems to qualify as any kind of road at all. We are a little worried, based on previous experience, about finding the south fork of this canyon. As it turns out, that isn't too difficult. A few miles up the canyon, there is a tank-sized boulder parked at the confluence of the south and north forks, with a discreet little sign to point the way: "Bear left."

**Resting along what once was a road in Trail Canyon**

We are rather hoping to get past the Morning Glory camp to the mines that are one and two miles past it up the canyon, but our going is so slow and tiring that we are happy just to reach the old camp before sunset. The camp buildings, despite being constructed without any regard for building codes and then neglected for the last fifty years, are a welcomed sight. There is a little cabin in a clearing on the side of the south slope, so we poke around inside.

In the cabin, there is a potbellied stove, table, a couple of chairs, and the steel frames and lattice remainders for three beds. On the shelves are an assortment of canned foods and half-full bottles of liquor, none of which are likely from this century. What was an attached bathroom has collapsed and is no longer functional. The walls and wood floor have gaps, one of the windows is broken out, and there is plenty of evidence of mouse habitation. Ah, home!

The temperature is falling below 40 degrees and clouds are moving in. We hardy souls may often sleep on the ground, but we agree that this cabin is a good place to spend tonight. We set about tidying up the place, claiming the beds (Johnny volunteers to take the floor), patching the window with plywood, and generally improving the abode to nearly the level of ramshackle.

After another fine meal of freeze-dried stuff that almost resembles what is shown on the package, we crawl into our sacks. We all agree that the spring lattice that supported a mattress on old steel bed frames works quite well with a hiking pad and sleeping bag over it. It seems, though, that people must have been several inches shorter before BJ and I were born.

We can hear the wind on the steel roof and the walls, which are a single layer of wood. We then hear the patter of a light rain, but in a few hours it becomes quiet. We sleep rather comfortably in our premium surroundings. All of us have to get up at some time of the night to go outside and relieve ourselves, and negotiating around Johnny's body in the meager remaining space of the floor is a bit of a challenge. Outside, it is really cold and there is a coating of snow on the ground. Ah, that is why the rain became quiet. In my opinion, it is great that we didn't have to sleep in the rain or snow, but surely Brad would have thought it bitchin'.

In the morning, we bundle up and poke around. There is a thermometer mounted on an outside wall that reads 34 degrees. The spring is only a hundred feet or so from the house, so we investigate and clean it so it will be more suitable to draw and filter water from later. We see a steel tank higher on the slope and scramble up to it. There is broken piping here leading to a higher outlet of the spring, but none of the equipment is salvageable without lots of tools and repair parts. We remain content with the lower spring. The seeping springs have made the whole slope lush with vegetation.

The original residents had some of the modern conveniences of life, including running water and a real bathroom with porcelain fixtures. On the front porch of the shack, we find a little toy truck constructed of a block of wood with nails for axles and can tops for wheels. A family lived here! That's why the cabin had some sense of home—and a restroom.

A homey little place
for a miner's family

It is phenomenal how a woman can incentivize a man to civility. In many cases, we've seen that it may be the only thing that works. The west was truly wild before enough women arrived to tame the testosterone and demand a more civilized society in exchange for their favors. Some hardy woman followed her man here to this beautiful but bleak canyon, while he tried to make it rich but only succeeded in making something of an existence for a while.

Also on site is a mostly collapsed bunkhouse, so there was more than just the family living in this camp. In that larger building is a 1950s stove and refrigerator, so there had been an electric generator here. We look inside what had been a shop with a twenty-foot-long workbench outside; we can tell that the shop was quite well equipped, and a few tools are still hanging. In a gully is the rusting hulk of a 1950s sedan (I think a Dodge) with its straight-six engine partially removed. The body is rusted, but the chrome grill still glints defiantly and looks as if it is grimacing. If this vehicle made the trip, the dirt road to Morning Glory camp was a lot smoother sixty years ago. A couple of ravens alight nearby, either curious or hopeful for food scraps. We rarely see birds away from Stovepipe Wells or Furnace Creek, but for ravens this is probably just a half-hour's cruise in the wind currents to those places.

Death Valley is perfect for giving perspective on human endeavors. The mining efforts here were on a relatively modest scale. Once abandoned, it would have taken only one good storm to obliterate the dirt road. Fifty or sixty years of sun, wind, rain, and snow half-demolished the wooden structures and rusted the steel. By the time they have been here for a hundred years, as evidenced at other sites in DVNP, all of the buildings will have collapsed and even the Dodge's chrome grill will have lost its sheen. After another hundred years and some good storms, there won't be much trace left of this camp and just a rust heap where the car was dumped. Nature shrugs off these small blemishes in what is short order by her scale. Even the most massive structures by humans will eventually become irrelevant, and our extensive destruction on earth will be erased by natural forces in a few millennia after we extinguish ourselves and most of the other species here. At least that's the way it now appears that humans are going. Nature's recovery process is a lesson that a geology degree will teach. It can probably also be learned by just observing what is happening in DVNP.

Even Detroit's best eventually surrenders to nature here.

The sun is out, the weather warms, and this time in DVNP is quiet, beautiful, and bright enough for us to appreciate the privilege of being alive in this place today. The shadows of the past are around us, but they only add definition to the magnificence of here, now. To the southwest we can see the snow-covered ridge where 9,000-foot Wildrose Peak is. That's not somewhere we will be going today.

In fact, we're not feeling particularly ambitious and there is a lot to explore nearby. While Johnny rests and reads in the luxury of our accommodations, BJ, Doogie, and I decide to walk a rough trail for a mile west to a small mine up the slope on the other side of the canyon. The mine's access adit is collapsed, so we rummage around in the tailings pile and enjoy the long view down Trail Canyon, sighting clear across Death Valley. It's a fine spot to have lunch.

When we return, the lower spring's catch basin is clear. We filter water to drink and then use the basin to splash faces and wash hands. We always appreciate it when we can have a clean face and hands in the middle of a DVNP hike. We go into the cabin to tidy it a bit more and make it even homier. We are doing nothing to slow the inevitable collapse of this cabin, just making it nicer until the structure is no longer safe to enter.

The night is cold again and we are grateful for the wood around, over, and under us. Maybe we are a bit less tired, because tonight we hear mice scurrying around in the dark. It makes sense that they would be here, with water and brush nearby and a ready-made structure to dwell under. We amicably share the building.

The next morning seems bittersweet. This is a comfortable place, and it feels like there are ambivalent or perhaps even benevolent spirits here. Maybe it is the relative newness of the structures compared to where we usually visit. People built a camp near a spring in a place with a fine view a mile or two from the three mines that were worked. In any case, today we have to pack everything up and load it onto our backs.

As always, walking down a wash isn't as tough as going up it. The canyon isn't magnificent, but it is far from ugly, so we have a pleasant hike with good friends. John and I alternate singing lines to a John Denver song at the top of our lungs. The canyon doesn't complain, and our two hiking buddies are at least tolerant. In most public places, that would not happen.

The Toyota is the first vehicle we reach, as it made it a bit higher up the wash. John and I walk down to the Honda and are loading it as we wave to Johnny and Brad driving by. We get in the Element, turn the key, and nothing happens—not even a click. BJ is so far gone that his dust cloud has settled. You can't bump-start a car with an automatic transmission, so we just wait.

After ten minutes or so, Brad realizes that there is nobody following, so he turns around and heads back as John and I have hoped he would. I have jumper cables, and with them, the Honda cranks over readily. We agree to stay together and stop at Furnace Creek, where I will see if the battery is charged enough to restart the car and just maybe figure out why it went dead.

In the Furnace Creek parking lot, the Honda does have enough battery charge to restart. I open the back hatch to dutifully pull out my tool kit, as if I actually knew what to look for. In lowering the tailgate, I notice that a catch for it has rattled loose, so I tighten that up. What luck! The loose catch had prevented the tailgate from closing completely, which kept the interior light on, which drained the battery over two days. With confidence that the battery will not go dead during the 400-mile drive home, we sigh with relief and exchange good-byes.

Voni maintains that the DVNP trips exact a toll on the reliability of the Element because of how it gets bounced and tested over unimproved roads. I go through a car wash on the way home, but it does not fool her.

She hasn't seen the extensive scraping of the undercarriage but has noticed that the left step rail is bent. Such is one of the hazards of marrying a very smart woman.

## Hiking Lessons

1. *As if we needed a reminder: hiking up a gravel wash is tough and slow.*

2. *This is common in Death Valley: What was a smooth dirt road that a passenger car could drive on degrades into a four-wheel-drive challenge and eventually becomes no road at all—just a route to hike along.*

3. *Having more than one vehicle is extremely helpful if you are driving somewhere to hike where nobody else is likely to go for days or weeks. There is no cell phone coverage in most of DVNP.*

4. *If you're pretty certain that nobody else is around, you can sing as loud as you want without worry of being embarrassed.*

## Life Lessons

1. *Like the miner's wife who tried to raise a family in Morning Glory, my wife has followed me dutifully to five jobs in three states. I am now painfully familiar with the sacrifices that a woman may make while supporting her man in his stubborn quest to try and achieve something highly meaningful. While trying to do better, I chased jobs and destabilized my disabled wife's security. Only recently have I come to realize the emotional price she paid.*

2. *Once outside of a tiny town like Mesquite, being a manager in a water district, or anything else, does not cause you to be a celebrity. Being anonymous again is actually welcomed. I can go to the store in a dirty shirt if I choose.*

3. *Morning Glory camp contains the ruins of things that were new when I was new. These were the physical products of people chasing their dreams. They are now crumbling remnants, and the names and lives of those people are forgotten. As I get closer to the end of my period on earth, I realize that despite our aspirations and efforts in younger years, the vast majority of us are, like the Death Valley*

*miners, destined to be forgotten, and the traces of our existence will also turn to dust. I now accept that the best almost all of us can hope for is a life that is positive and that only collectively can we perhaps evolve our species to a healthier state. I believe that it's more the billions of small acts of thoughtful kindness that shape our world than the heroic or genius moments of a few. I will never be one of those few geniuses, but without the shifts from a billion of our small actions, the brilliant and magnificent insights could not be realized. Yes, there are still broken, wicked, corrupt, stupid, and destructive people. Unfortunately, maybe humans need that perspective to recognize the good that is around. Without darkness, could we appreciate the light?*

# 2015

# Titanothere Canyon & Titus Canyon

*Really Memorable Nights*

After several Brad-inspired cross-country loops, I thought of trying my hand at designing one, and the guys acquiesced. Maybe they were hoping for an easier trip. As it turns out, that would have been false hope.

Titanothere Canyon seems interesting and remote, but hiking almost 5,000 feet up seems arduous and bordering impossible. Hiking down it looks possible. Avoiding an up-and-back trek means that we will have to leave a vehicle at one end, hike down to it, and then drive back to the other vehicle at the top. The next canyon to the north is Titus Canyon, which has a one-way road down it. It would take too long to also walk Titus on this trip, but Digonnet promises that it has plenty to explore, including Leadfield, a 1927 ghost town. Brad says that author John Soennichsen warns not to stay overnight in Leadfield, as it is haunted and creepy.

So, the idea is to spend two days descending Titanothere and the third day exploring and driving down Titus. I believe that walking twelve miles down a canyon, down an alluvial fan, to a paved road with a bright orange car parked on it should be possible without getting lost. Well, theoretically.

We meet at Stovepipe Wells to start, as always arriving just a few minutes from each other. The weather is 70 degrees and cloudless. Brad is driving a Nissan sedan this year, having read that Titus Canyon Road is usually passable with a passenger car. We drive both cars north on Scotty's Castle Road and park the Element where it seems that Digonnet has suggested. Next, we practice one of those circus clown performances where an impossible amount of stuff fits into a car. Since a fully loaded backpack is about the size of a small child, we have the equivalent of eight people inside the trunk and cabin of a mid-sized sedan.

The drive to the top of Titanothere Canyon is about thirty miles on a paved road and then ten miles on a one-way smooth dirt road. We find the place Digonnet tells us to park above the top of Titanothere, grateful that he described it well because we wouldn't have guessed that this is the right spot otherwise. This one-way road means that overshooting it would be an inconvenience at best. So far, so good. We are also grateful to spill out of our cramped enclosure. We haven't seen another car on this dirt road.

Our drive has been a steady climb to 5,000' elevation. This high rolling plain with peaks poking out of it is all scrub brush. This elevation is, on average, more than 20 degrees cooler than the valley floor, so moisture evaporates less rapidly, helping vegetation to survive. There is also more precipitation in the mountains, and today this highland does not feature the cloudless, mild weather we experienced this morning at Stovepipe Wells. We need jackets here, and it seems as if it could rain at any time.

Titanothere Canyon is down between those two peaks.

This is a revealing moment for our group philosophy. In consideration of the weather, we could have rethought the itinerary, perhaps driving down Titus Canyon today and spending the night in the dry valley. The next day we could have started the two-day hike down Titanothere, anticipating a weather change. We could have thought about how uncomfortable tonight might be in a rainy Titanothere Canyon since we didn't bring tents and there are no mines or buildings in the whole canyon to hide in. Yes, we might have considered these things. Instead, we just shoulder our packs and walk west, looking for the top of the canyon to descend. We have a way of creating our own adventures by planning trips that are inherently filled with challenges and then adding some more challenges through our behaviors. To be fair to the other guys, most of the fate-tempting decision-making on this trip was my doing, and they just went along with it.

It seems like the canyon must be between the two peaks just west of us, beyond which we can see the Panamint Mountains some thirty miles distant. Wow, this hike starts with a very nice, smooth, and gradual downhill. That lasts for all of a couple of hundred yards and will be the only easy walking for two days. We soon come to the edge of the canyon, surprisingly abrupt at its top. Yep, this is the place. I don't know if John and Johnny are wondering now what I've gotten us into, but I am. Brad is probably stoked—the tougher the better for him.

The descent starts serious but walkable for a way. We soon come to an eighty-foot drop-off, which Digonnet says can be easily circumvented by a "boulder-strewn talus slope on its west side." Knowing Digonnet's capabilities and what a boulder-strewn talus slope can mean for us in terms of traversing, I might have taken more pause before selecting this route. We move slowly behind Brad; even he has to stop at a point where climbing with hands will be required to descend the next ten feet. We gather and decide that descending is only reasonably possible if we lower our packs and poles separately. We shed our gear and Brad climbs down first, of course. I'm the guy who gets to lower the packs, while Johnny and John nervously observe. The first couple of backpacks go OK, although there isn't much space for them once they get to BJ. Next is John's pack, which is one of the heaviest. Somehow, between a lack of space or a slip, we drop the pack.

You'd think that a heavily loaded backpack with sleeping bag would just flop over and lay flat on a slope, even a pretty steep one. Maybe it would roll a bit. None of us expected that it could cartwheel. At any second it should stop. It couldn't possibly spin like that down 200 feet to the bottom of this ravine, could it? Yes, apparently it could.

It would be hilarious—if the pack didn't hold all of Doogie's stuff and it wasn't at the bottom of a ravine. The halting conversation goes something like this:

Brad: "Oh. Wow."

Johnny: "I didn't know a backpack could cartwheel that well."

Ken: "Sure is a long way down."

John: "I hope the crackers aren't broken."

We might as well keep the mood light. Everyone gets safely down the drop in their own fashion. Brad and I prefer to face the cliff and climb down. John and Johnny like to slide down on their butts whenever they can, preferring to keep an eye on their fates. Johnny's shorts begin to tear. Once we move downslope a way further, BJ and I figure out how to descend to the base of the ravine and retrieve John's pack. Amazingly, it looks like nothing on the outside has torn or come off. Doogie, in perpetual good humor, just shrugs his load back on.

The scenery in this deep v canyon is good, but the thickening cloud cover keeps us from seeing very far. There are another couple of rock chutes to descend, but nothing as scary as the one we just came through. Johnny continues to slide down them. By the time we are two miles into the hike, Johnny's left butt cheek is showing through his torn pants. I hadn't previously thought of tearing one's pants as a reason not to slide down rocks, but maybe it is a legitimate consideration, at least if you are going to be around other people.

Now, in midafternoon, it is beginning to rain. We see a big boulder, so we take one of our plastic sheets, throw it over the boulder, and anchor it. This creates a cover where we can crouch against the boulder on the lee side. It mostly works, although the crowding is about like it was in Brad's sedan. In less than an hour, before we can wonder how we will spend the night here, the rain abates. Hoping for a better alternative, we continue walking down-canyon, looking for rain protection.

Digonnet speaks of the remnants of a rock shelter 2.7 miles from the top of the canyon on the eastern side, so we seek that as the only reasonable option to minimize our exposure to more rain. After managing to sleep in cabins for the last few trips, we think this isn't looking as favorable. We do find the location, although the spot doesn't have much left that would qualify as a shelter. There is one flat-sided boulder several feet high and about ten feet long. At each end, two low rows of loose stones tumble out at right angles. As it begins to rain again, we rapidly rebuild the end walls as best as we can, clear out the space between them, and with whatever rocks we can find, construct a very low wall a few feet out from the big wall. The backpacks make up part of this outside wall. With all of our plastic sheets we make a cover for the clearing, supported by rope strung across the rocks.

Underneath the low cover, Johnny and Brad have their heads at one end and unroll their bags. John and I do the same at the other end. The four bags overlap in the middle. It is even tighter than it was in the car driving up here. We are more dry than wet, at least. Every twenty minutes or less, one of us has to reach up from our sacks to the underside of the plastic roof, pushing the ponded water to the downside, where it runs off. This goes on all night in the steadiest rain we have ever encountered in DVNP. It is easy to gauge the rain intensity when it patters on a sheet of plastic twenty inches over your head.

Most nights are easily forgotten, as they are fairly comfortable and slept through. This night is...memorable.

A night with close friends under a sheet of plastic

Shortly before daybreak, the rain stops. We emerge in pretty good cheer. We now get to sit outside and have breakfast, take down the shelter, and lay out and pack our gear, all without rain! There are low clouds bridging the canyon and hiding the mountain crests, so we can't see far, but what we can see is moist and clean. We're not exactly refreshed, but we are happy and optimistic because we are not soaked and frozen.

This canyon hike was my idea, so in consideration of our current location and the fact that the lower elevations get much less rain, I suggest a plan: We are still nine miles away and nearly 4,000 feet higher in elevation than the lower car. It will take a full day to hike down to the road, drive that car up to the car at the top, then find tonight's campsite on the way to Leadfield, the ghost town near the top of Titus Canyon. With the clouds, we can't see the mountains around us to explore anyway, so let's just concentrate on walking downhill. Because Johnny is struggling with his worsening knees and is walking slowly, I suggest we all take something heavy from his pack so that he can better hobble down this trailless expanse to the lower car. If we simply go down this canyon and the alluvial fan, we will intersect with Scotty's Castle Road, where the car is. Since the Element is bright orange, we should be able to see it from some distance. It seems like a good plan to the others. This goes pretty well for miles. BJ surges ahead with John in his wake. I hang back with Johnny. When Brad and John stop, Johnny and I catch up to them and admire the improving scenery. As the clouds clear, we can eventually see a dramatic feature on the south canyon wall called Pinnacles, and we come to a narrows that Digonnet calls "The Neck." This canyon is called Titanothere after a fossil found here of a rhinoceros-sized beast that roamed 40 million years ago when the region was wetter and featured low hills and lakes. Unfortunately, we don't have time or energy to search for fossils today.

As the canyon gets wider, the strata in the walls become more dramatic and tilted. With a wider canyon, the possible paths become more numerous due to the alternate water courses in a broader basin approximating the top of an alluvial fan. The view also continues to broaden as the mouth of the canyon gets closer. Johnny and I catch up to John and Brad several times, but toward the mouth of the canyon, we have lost sight of them again. I have steered Johnny in a path to the south side of the canyon because I believe that the car is at the south side of the alluvial fan's base. We stop to rest where the canyon wall abruptly ends. At this point, the washes are about ten feet deep and are broad and numerous. Although this seems to Johnny and me like an obvious place to stop, our partners are nowhere in sight. We can tell where the two-lane road must be on the valley floor, but we can't actually see it, since it's over three miles away. We know that alluvial fans are not easy to walk on, even downhill, so we quietly rest for a little while and have a snack.

It seems to us that John and Brad must have gone ahead, so we expect to find them on this alluvial fan. Unbeknownst to us, they have stopped in this general area, but in some other deep wash, hidden from view. Although he is limping in pain with every step, Johnny keeps moving. He does not complain and lets me slowly pick a path for us.

As I've mentioned in every previous encounter with alluvial fans, they are no pleasure to walk on. The countless braided courses where water has come down mean that there are no straight lines, the footing is unstable, and no little stream bed lasts for long before it goes sideways or ends. At least our direction today is downhill. Our hiking sticks prevent many falls on this surface, which is the extreme opposite of what is appropriate for walking.

Because we have to watch every step here, we have to stop to look around for our friends. We rest and search every half mile. The scenery is vast below this alluvial fan, and we can see a large swath of Death Valley. The sky is now cloudless. The view is spectacular. We figure it is most likely that

Doogie and BJ are ahead of us and too far away to see. Maybe they decided to speed all of the way down to the road and wait there. In any case, the option of backtracking and looking for them isn't viable, with Johnny's knees being bad and the chance of finding them uphill getting slimmer as the hours add up. At least John and Brad are together, so if one of them is injured the other can come down to find us at the car and we can put together a rescue. It was an alluvial fan like this that made me break my leg ten years ago. We are all smarter than I was then, now possessing walking sticks and boots, so a fall is less likely.

My initial intention is to bear southwest, towards where the still-not-visible car must be. After less than a mile, I change the strategy to just going as straight downhill to the road as is practical, minimizing our steps on this unfriendly surface. If I have to walk a mile or more south on the road to get to the car, it is worth the trade-off. Eventually we see the road below and an orange glint to the southwest, so the plan is confirmed. Johnny keeps limping along, not complaining about his physical condition, but worried about our friends. I use my best rationalizations to try and calm his concerns.

By early afternoon, we step on the road shoulder and unload our packs. There is no sign of the other guys, but they could be at the car. Johnny has walked nine miles on rough terrain with a big pack and bad knees. "Tough" hardly comes close to describing him. He is comfortable resting here, so I head south on the road, walking at a Brad-like speed because I'm on a smooth surface and unburdened by a pack. It takes only fifteen minutes to reach the car, and the other guys are not there. I drive back to Johnny, who is grateful but still alone. We are perplexed but not hopeless.

We drive north for a few miles, then south, fifteen miles back to Stovepipe Wells, thinking that they may have hitched a ride there. Nothing. We drive back north on Scotty's Castle Road, miles past the north side of the Titanothere alluvial fan. Nothing. We turn around and slowly drive south on Scotty's Castle Road, which is no problem because there are no other cars. We scan the alluvial fan and honk the car horn every half minute. Johnny is very worried, and I'm getting nervous as well. Midway along the base of the fan, I see them in the distance, waving their sticks high. What a relief!

Their story is that after waiting and not seeing us at the mouth of the canyon, BJ and Doogie became concerned and backtracked about a mile, to where they had last seen us. They then headed again down the canyon and fan, looking for us the whole way. Considering that they had walked a couple of miles further than Johnny and me and should be tired, they moved very briskly at the sight of our vehicle. I guess that this sort of event is inevitable if we are splitting up to hike at different speeds without a trail.

It is now about 4:00 p.m. and we still have some driving to do. The Element has only a little more room inside than the sedan, but any vehicle would be welcomed at this point. The drive up to Brad's car is uneventful but punctuated with many thankful comments about the safe outcome. Like yesterday, there are no other vehicles, and the scenery is magnificent in the waning light. By the time we get to the other car, it is nearly dark. We decide to keep to our plan, even though we could just camp where we are. We don't want to go clear to Leadfield tonight; we vaguely remember it's reported to have bad vibes. I'd forgotten how Digonnet mentions that this one-way dirt road becomes winding and steep, descending 1,100 feet to Leadfield a few miles to the north. Let's add no guard rails, muddy, and pitch black to the current conditions. I drive timidly and very slowly.

Again, I have led these guys into what they might generously refer to as a continuing adventure. We continue to where the road becomes flatter with some room to pull over, and we decide that is far enough for now. It is completely dark, we can't tell where we are, and we don't want to overshoot our target. You aren't supposed to camp near the road in DVNP, but in the current situation, we are out of other options.

John, Johnny, and I have had enough bedding adventures for one trip. It is cold and the black sky means that there is a cloud cover. John and I elect to sleep in the Element, which can accommodate full length bedding through an interior design that allows the front seat backs to recline level with the rear seats. Johnny is the shortest and is happy to curl up on the back bench seat of the sedan. Brad never seems to maximize his adventure saturation index and elects to sleep on the ground. We have the vehicles' lights to see well enough to eat and set up our sleeping arrangements, but we can't see anything that might tell us where we are.

If you are old enough to have dated at drive-in movies, then you know how steamy a car interior can get if closed up on a cold night. It is still humid with the windows cracked open, but we have a much more comfortable night's sleep in the cars than we had under a sheet of plastic in the rain. When we arise somewhat refreshed in the morning, we can see that it has not rained again, but there is frost on Brad's sleeping bag. For three of us, it was a happy choice to have taken the less adventurous alternative and slept in a car.

The morning sun reveals that we have blindly chosen a scenic spot. The mountain peaks to the northwest have a dusting of snow, quickly melting

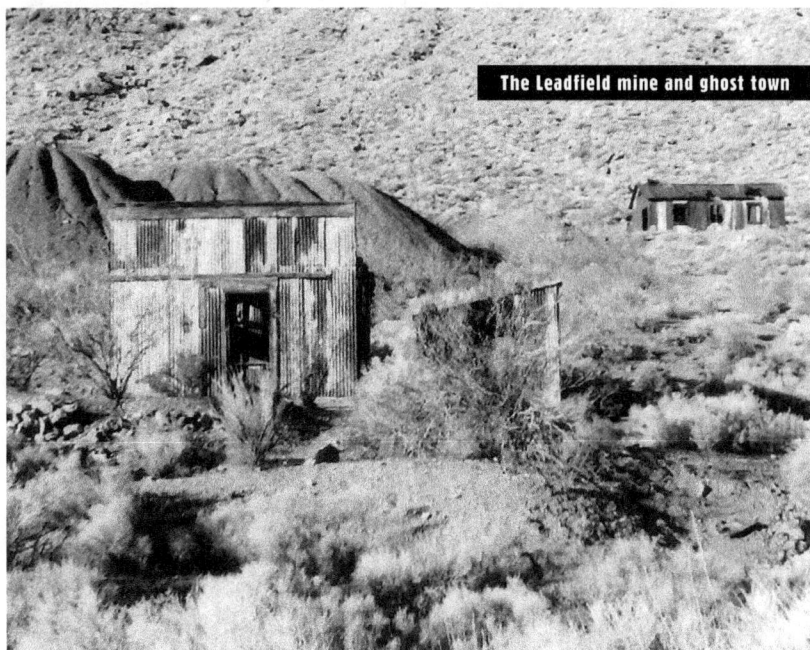

The Leadfield mine and ghost town

away as the sun rises. Sprinkled around us are the buildings of the ghost town Leadfield. In our excitement, we had forgotten about the Leadfield ghost stories.

It is not until five years later that Johnny reveals to me that he was tormented with nightmares that night. In his dreams, he was either in San Francisco trying to justify to the state that he could sell shares in the mine or here at Leadfield trying to encourage development. That is eerily close to the story that Soennichsen tells in *Live from Death Valley* of Jack Salsberry, the promoter who started this mine and town. Leadfield was a boom town started in 1925. It quickly acquired fifty mining claims and even established its own post office and newspaper. The main lead vein also yielded silver and the mine tunnel was soon 600 feet long. By January 1927, though, the town was essentially abandoned. Talk about a fast boom and bust.

As for this morning, we can barely wait to finish breakfast before walking around to explore the structures. The buildings are constructed of widely spaced rough studs spanned with corrugated steel. They seem safe enough to walk through carefully, but we wouldn't spend a night in one. Well, maybe we would, if it was raining and we didn't know about the haunted Leadfield stories. We climb up the tailings heap to the mine's opening on the hillside. The mine has crumbling walls and timbers, so we decline to explore inside. Doogie sits in the tailings and uses his hand lens to study the rock fragments for minerals. He still remembers from our mineralogy class the names and appearances of minerals that I mostly forgot by the time UCSB handed me a degree.

We appreciate the beautiful setting and views here, although that aspect likely mattered little or not at all to the residents ninety years ago. We spend a few hours poking around, initially being in no hurry to leave something unseen. Finally, we all admit that this whole place feels creepy, and we decide to move on. We have a picturesque canyon drive promised ahead and, following that, our long drives home, so we have logical reasons to climb back into the cars.

If you are a real geologist, then Titus Canyon would be a place to spend weeks. The tilting of layers is greater than the slope of the canyon floor, so the strata are younger down-canyon and are over 500 million years old at the top. There is extreme folding of rock layers in some places.

For the other 99 percent of us, the general impression is just that the colorful strata and steep walls make the canyon awesome. In the several long narrows, the walls are nearly vertical and up to 500 feet high. It is the only place that I've encountered where one can drive a car through such dramatic narrows. It is jaw-dropping. Speaking of driving a car, Brad's sedan does make it down, but not without powering it aggressively through the

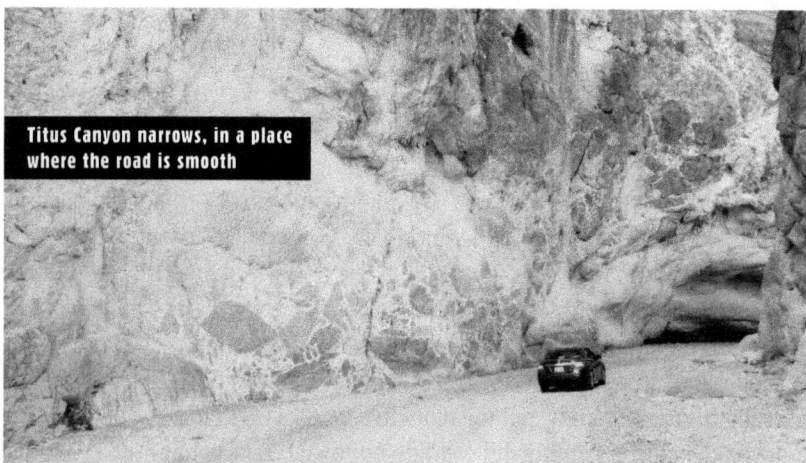

Titus Canyon narrows, in a place where the road is smooth

deeper gravel sections so that it doesn't bog down...and not without some undercarriage scraping. For non-Brads, I'd say that a passenger car here is not recommended.

A mile or so from the top of the canyon is Klare Spring, the only source of year-round water in this whole canyon. It is a typical DVNP spring—meager in output, with the water quickly disappearing into the sand below. Plants grow around this wet crack in the rock wall, and animal tracks are in the mud.

Above the spring is a modest rock panel of petroglyphs left by Native Americans. My genealogy says that I'm exclusively of western European descent, but I feel a pull to the land and culture of Native Americans. Their lives were connected with the environment in a way that is unimaginably intimate to most current Americans. John, Brad, Johnny, and I get a touch of the Native American's ancient reality through our hikes, although we are augmented with nylon backpacks and freeze-dried dinners. The petroglyphs we study help us to better strengthen the connection to our native brethren. I am closer in time and culture to the miners who dug up the hills and left their unnatural blemishes wherever they went, but my spirit is with the indigenous people.

We've had a morning exploring what men wrought in two years in Lead-field, and then we reveled in the beauty from millions of years of nature's crafting in the canyon. A profane and sacred juxtaposition. It is early afternoon when we get to the bottom of Titus Canyon. It will be about 9:00 p.m. when I arrive home in Arizona, bone tired.

It is good to have the wife and creature comforts with a head full of memories for another year.

## Hiking Lessons

1.  *A tightly stuffed modern backpack can cartwheel downhill two hundred feet without being significantly damaged. Some crackers inside may get broken, though.*

2.  *When hiking without trails, it is perhaps best to not lose sight of each other unless you are in a very narrow canyon.*

3.  *Each hiker should bring a whistle and blow it when they can't find their companions.*

4.  *If you are going to hike separately, agreeing on a plan for where you are headed helps.*

5.  *If you do split up, keep at least two in each group.*

6.  *Pay close attention to your guide's (in our case, Digonnet's) written directions to avoid potential challenges—unless you welcome them all.*

7.  *If you are going to slide down rock chutes on your butt, bring a second pair of pants.*

## Life Lessons

1.  *Being creative, resourceful, and persistent helps when handling challenging situations.*

2.  *Being flexible on the sequence of plans—for example, doing Leadfield and Titus Canyon first—might have made it possible to spend every night without rain. Then again, it seems that part of the purpose of our adventures is to have these challenges.*

3.  *Most nights spent sleeping at home or in motels are forgotten. Most nights spent sleeping outside are not. Especially if it rains.*

4.  *If people say a place is haunted, it probably is. Why would they make that stuff up?*

5.  *Petroglyphs are a mystery to most modern people, but while recently viewing some in Arizona, my son offered a reasonable explanation: they are mostly advertisements. For example, a depiction of an archer could simply mean, "Get your arrows at Pointy's!"*

# 2016

# Lower Marble Canyon, Deadhorse Canyon, & Journigan's Mill

*Same Place, Completely Changed*

This year, we return to the west side of the Panamint Mountains, which run north-south on the south side of DVNP. In anticipation of some higher elevation camping—and remembering last year—we plan for a bit more warmth by going in early March instead of January or February. All of our adventures this year will be day hikes from a car camp, meaning that we return to that base each evening. We are avoiding overnight backpacking because Johnny is having progressively more trouble distance walking due to his degrading knees, and I can't carry a heavy pack because of a compromised left shoulder. It's great to be part of a team that is so considerate!

We meet as usual for breakfast at Stovepipe Wells. Our plan for the first day is to hike the same lower Marble Canyon that we ascended on our first group trip, in 2003. We are also intending purposely to go back up Deadhorse Canyon, which was a mistake the first year, but a beautiful one.

Brad's older son, Stone, is now 19 years old and has joined us on this trip. He's not really conversational at first, perhaps intimidated by his father's tales of those studs he hikes with and our dangerous exploits. Stone appears plenty fit enough for this group. As time passes, he becomes more confident and conversant.

What are the chances that a Rock and a Stone end up hiking together?

The first year that we went up Marble Canyon we used a minivan, which carried us to the end of the dirt road where the rough gravel road starts. This year, Brad is driving a Jeep SUV, which takes the last 2.6 gravel miles in stride. John joins me in my Honda Element, a car that aspires to be an SUV if it only had more ground clearance, power, and four-wheel drive. Driving cautiously but persistently while tolerating the loud noises from rocks hitting the undercarriage, we also make it up to the mouth of the canyon.

Wow, we have great camping here near the parked cars at 1,800' elevation. For us, great means scenic. There are no RV hookups—or RVs, for that matter. No electricity, water, restrooms, shade, or even tables. Just a beautiful view of the foot of the Panamint Mountains, with flat sand for sleeping that is elevated above the road. We are also grateful that we didn't have to walk that last gravel section like we did thirteen years ago and still remember well. There are a few other SUVs and trucks scattered here, indicating perhaps that temperate weather brings more visitors.

"Glad we weren't here when the flash flood did this."

We shoulder light day packs and enter the canyon. There has been a dramatic change in Marble Canyon. Where we had struggled on sand and gravel, there is now a smooth surface of hard-packed clay. In the clay are random half-inch wide cracks with plants, some of them a foot high and flowering. There are a few rather large mushrooms sprouting up as well. The formerly clean polished walls have sections splattered with dirt. The most spectacular splatter is in a carved-out section large enough to park a car, plastered with mud up to fifteen feet above the canyon deck.

On our 2003 hike, we had contemplated how the canyon's erosion was a by-product of flash flooding, and we made sure to camp in a location that would give us an escape if we heard one coming. Now we're back in the aftermath of a recent flood, surveying the effects. The clay deposited by the flood has provided a moist reserve that has spawned large flowering plants that we have never seen in DVNP before. It has also provided a nearly perfect walking surface, beating almost any prepared trail. This sort of a walk in a DVNP canyon seems otherworldly.

Thanks to the favorable conditions, Johnny makes it past the first narrows and up to the petroglyphs. The remarkable petroglyphs are high enough to have been untouched by the latest flood or seemingly by any flood in the last several centuries. After spending time with the petroglyphs, we continue up the canyon and Johnny heads back to the cars. With nothing but narrows between this spot and the cars, we're certain that we'll see him later today. The hiking is remarkably easy with backpacks of nominal weight on this soft pavement of smooth, dry clay. This is really nice.

We pass the junction where we now know that Marble Canyon would continue and take the left leg to go up Deadhorse Canyon. At the place where we formerly found bighorn sheep bones, we find more of them, clean of any meat. Knowing that the flash flood recently washed out or buried everything that was here, this is clear confirmation that the spot is a cougar kill zone. Wow, you'd have to be a desperate sheep to drink here. The falls that were wet and frozen before are now dry and barren of bushes. We can see what gene pool Stone came from, as he climbs the fall like his father. John and I manage, more slowly and less gracefully.

The area above the fall that was clogged with brush now has a lot less of it, having been thinned by the flood. At about 3,500' elevation, we stop for lunch in the shade of some scrubby trees. It would be nice to get to the top, but we decide that if we go much further up the canyon, we may not get back to camp before dark.

The descent down the falls is a bit challenging, but thanks to the smooth walking surface the rest of the hike out is relaxing, considering that we've been moving all day. Johnny is waiting for us at the camp as the sun drops behind the mountains and the camp is bathed in shadow. We all admonish him for not having set up our sleeping sites or prepared dinner with cold beers. Drive a man to a desolate place to abandon him, and that's the thanks you get.

We get a quiet and beautiful night that is just cool enough to make the sleeping bag welcomed.

The next morning, we pile into the vehicles and drive out on the dirt road, doing some playful sliding in the sand. We head to the rarely used but well-paved Emigrant Canyon Road. This next base camp will be at about 4,375' elevation.

Next to Emigrant Canyon Road are the remains of Journigan's ore processing mill—concrete foundations, mostly. It is a nice flat area with an easy dirt drive to the paved road. We decide to set our camp a little way away from the six round concrete pads that were the bases for the cyanide tanks used in gold ore separating between the 1930s and 1950s. Cyanide is highly poisonous and is still used today in gold ore processing. We can tell that this isn't the first time that someone has camped here, but today we have the place to ourselves. Just now I've figured out that the road was probably paved because of the now-defunct mines and ore processing operation that were active relatively recently, in Death Valley historical terms. There is no other significant destination on this road.

Digonnet describes how this mill site was selected because of its access to plentiful spring water, piped down from areas uphill. Those springs are the destination for today's hike. Since it is promised to be without trails, steep, and at times brush-blocked, Johnny is going to stay in the camp. The weather here is beautiful, the views splendid, and as it turns out, there are plenty of artifacts for Johnny to explore and show us later. That still leaves four of us to hike, which our experience indicates is enough to figure out how to get out of where we are lost or deal with somebody's injuries. We elders all have the *Hiking Death Valley* book with Digonnet's description and his map of a cross-country loop towards Jayhawker Canyon to the west and back to this camp, so we shouldn't get lost, at least. Yeah, right.

We load food, water, and a few other things into relatively light backpacks and hit the non-trail by about 10:00 a.m. It quickly gets steep, but not crawling-up steep. There are some interesting hoodoos on the canyon slope, formed by erosion around large rocks that end up topping columns of easily eroded material. We come to an overgrown area with lots of water that requires some perseverance to get past. We think it is Malapi Spring. Maybe so, or as it turns out in retrospect, maybe it is Canyon Spring. In any case, it is hard to read the terrain with all this brush, so we keep going uphill in what we think is the main drainage. This repeats a lesson in drainage deception that we should have learned from our very first hike in DVNP. The going is slow, and every hundred yards feels like a mile. I greatly admire Michel Digonnet but at the moment am not very pleased with his interpretation of a nice day hike. As usual, it is my frustration with my own limitations that colors my perception.

In any case, in a few hundred yards/several miles, we come to the end of the drainage at a box canyon. A box canyon means there is no clear path up in any direction, a sign to anyone but certain fools to give up. We decide, mostly at my urging, to climb to the top a few hundred feet higher in elevation, because we can't tell in this hole where we are on the map. Topo maps are a lot easier to interpret from high ground because you can see further. Before there is much time for dissent or logic, I begin crawling up the grade, warning everyone to beware of falling loose rocks.

Brad and Stone don't have much trouble clambering. We're rather sorely testing John, who gently says later that he thought we might die there. (Without making me feel like a total ass, John supplies us with a retrospective of how a more sensible person might assess a situation.) In twenty or thirty minutes, after some tense situations, we reach the top. It is a walkable ridge with a couple of high points and a spectacular view. This is a truly splendid place to have lunch, made better because we are all alive, albeit currently lost. I hope to have not helped lead this team into disaster, because none of us think that returning down that grade is a good idea. It is time to act confident but intensely study the topo map and find a way out of this fix. Lunch is our first priority, though. We are at 5,500' elevation, according to the altimeter. It is so pristine up here that we can convince ourselves that we are the first to visit this spot, aside from ravens. We can see a deep canyon to our west. Miles to the south the hills disappear and Death Valley begins. The deeply furrowed terrain to the east is where we think we should be headed.

This mountaintop is distinctive. With the compass, altimeter, and Brad's GPS, we find our location on the map. I can hardly believe not only that we are a ravine too far to the north, but also that Digonnet's suggested cross-country path traverses a contour below a crest and past two other ravines before descending into a third. That guy was half mountain goat! It didn't look so bad on the topographic map, but from this high point it looks like it would be nearly as hard as crawling up the box canyon—and a hell of a lot farther. As we all look at the terrain and map, we have more than a little concern at the prospect of continuing the route we initially intended.

Fortunately, there appears to be another way out of here. We can follow this crest south and gradually drop into the drainage where Malapi Spring should exist, which is where Digonnet directed us in the first place, not intending for us to climb quite this high. We agree that this now makes the most sense. I'm happy with the lesson that Stone is getting—not the one where the old guys make mistakes and get lost, but the one about how we work together to get out of the situation.

As our hopes increase and our heart rates stabilize, I remember that I've brought something special. Recently a young man in our neighborhood, in his despair, committed suicide. His family painted his name on a box full of smooth river-polished cobbles, asking that in his memory we take these stones to special places. In this way he will have travelled so much more in spirit than he did in his abbreviated life. I climb a short way to the top of this mountain and place the polished stone on the craggy summit, saying a short and clumsy prayer for Nic. Assuming we hikers return in one piece down our new route, it now seems that climbing to this mountaintop was a beautiful, fortuitous mistake.

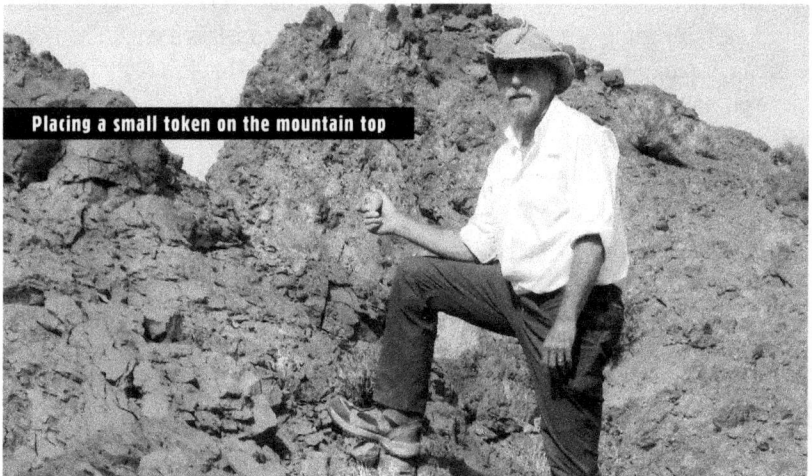

Placing a small token on the mountain top

Most of our descending now can be done standing normally with the walking sticks extended several inches so that they reach out ahead and down from our steps. There are some steeper places, but not terribly so. Some narrows are clogged with brush, as Digonnet described. We arrive in a shaded rocky narrow where Malapi Spring delivers clear, cool water at about ten to twenty gallons per minute into a shallow rock pool. This is a lot of flow for a DVNP spring. We all soak our feet and splash our faces here, enjoying the accomplishment because we are pretty sure that we know where we are and how to return.

There is more climbing down and bushwhacking, and we arrive at the place where we missed our turn on the way up. It is entirely understandable, as this ravine's connection is hidden with overgrowth. There aren't many places in DVNP where a path is choked off with plant growth—it's amazing what a steady flow of water can cause. The next mile down is uneventful, and it is always a relief to get confirmation that you are on a familiar route, headed back to your starting point.

It is midafternoon, and John and I are in need of a rest. Stone and Brad appear barely fazed. Johnny has discovered some interesting things while we were getting lost, so after a fair break he leads us a few hundred meters around the area. He has found several rusty, gutted vehicles, all somewhat older, even, than me. This is an interesting place to poke around and take photos. New cars, with all of their plastic, would not look so intact after seventy years of abandonment.

We have our usual dinner of rehydrated camp chow. Each package is supposed to have two servings but each of us never fails to each finish our own package. Maybe we did get Brad and Stone a little tired, because by 7:15 p.m. everyone is in the sacks, reading or stargazing. I see a meteor streak past.

The next morning, we pack up completely and drive a half mile up Emigrant Canyon Road to where a former dirt road intersects it. This hasn't been a passable road in several decades, but it is still a fair trail by DVNP standards. We shoulder light day packs and all five of us walk the mile-plus to the site of the Greene and Detloff mill. There are quite a few old buildings and vehicles to explore here.

This gold ore crushing mill, like most other mines and ore mills in DVNP, had a short but intense life. What is left here is a single-room bunkhouse with three beds, an outhouse, and the large wood and sheet metal structure that enclosed the mill. Imagine hauling everything here from the nearest town of consequence, easily over a hundred miles away. You can't pop on over to Lowe's for lumber, Home Depot for some brackets, or Ace Hardware because a two-inch screw would work better than the two-and-a-half-inch

The mill building will not be standing much longer.

ones that you have. These structures were made simply and cheaply with large gauge wood, big nails, and sheet metal. The residential structure has the first gypsum wallboard that we've seen in DVNP.

The big mill is sketchy to walk in, as it looks like the roof and walls could finish their collapse with little provocation. The house is still mostly intact, so we can see how the residents lived. There are some commodities on the shelves—most no doubt from later visitors—but none of it appealing or young enough for us to sample.

These buildings, like many of the structures we visit in DVNP, seem haunted by the energies of those passion-crazed men who invested all that they had in the hopes that they'd strike it rich. They dreamed of what was possible, believing that they could be, should be, and would be that clever SOB who beat the odds and became a mining baron. Their fantasies fueled them, even as they resorted to cannibalizing many of the vehicles that got them here. When reality came crashing in, it must have been a harsh awakening. The generator and ore-crushing equipment here were taken by the next men with gold-dazzled hopes, but almost nothing else that they had brought in was worth carrying out. There was no time, money, morality, legal requirement, or energy to protect the structures or cover the mines. They just rolled away in their last functioning vehicles.

OK, each of them did take away something. They took back stories of how they were gold miners in Death Valley and made it work for a few years. It is likely that nobody else around them would have something comparable to talk about from their life histories. I would have listened to those stories.

We spend a couple of hours taking pictures and have lunch in the serene and beautiful, but sobering, setting before walking back to our vehicles.

Brad's Jeep has a tire with a slow leak, so everyone else piles into my car to go back to the gas station at Stovepipe Wells and air up the tire. In all of our trips to DVNP, we have never seen as many cars and people as there are today at Stovepipe Wells. There had been significant rains this winter, and the spring weather has caused a profusion of flowers to pop up in the usually barren desert. With the flowers and mild weather come more tourists. Almost none of them will venture off the paved roads, but they will all have fine photos and stories of beautiful vistas in DVNP. I get some good flower pictures on my way out as well. In two days, I'll get my bum shoulder operated on and be ready for next year.

## Hiking Lessons

1.  *Using a car as a base camp can be pretty sweet and allow you to cover more ground.*

2.  *You can hike and climb much better without a heavy pack. That slope in the box canyon could not have been climbable if we had full packs.*

3.  *You're never too well prepared to not get lost. Well, at least we aren't.*

4.  *It is important to be resourceful and have good companions when things go awry.*

## Life Lessons

1.  *Character matters. Great buddies make it possible to have a good time even when you have compromising physical conditions.*

2.  *Time changes some things, even in Death Valley.*

3.  *Beware of magic genies such as ones disguised as a gold mine opportunity too good to pass up.*

4.  *It is important to be resourceful and have good companions when things go awry.*

## 2017

# Joshua Tree National Park

### *The Motor and Me*

I initiate the idea of a trip to the Racetrack area for early February, which BJ embraces. That time doesn't work for either John or Johnny, due to personal issues. If they need to forego the therapeutic value of a DVNP trip, then something important must be happening.

Brad says that he can bring along his two teenaged sons. Having previously hiked with Stone, I know that there is nothing I can do that he can't, but quite likely a lot he can do (like his father), which will be beyond me. The slightly younger son is reportedly just as athletic. My wife has a strong premonition that something will go wrong with me trying to keep up with three much younger and daring accomplices, especially without John and Johnny to help slow the pace. I've learned not to question her about these things. (Remember the broken leg fiasco when I ignored her warning?) I wish Brad well, and he says after returning that they had a great trip and would like to show the area to our team. Problems comes up at work for me anyway, so maybe that was the source of Voni's premonition? In any case, February leaves me intact and grateful to my wife.

I float the idea for a reschedule in March when my wife has a trip to Disneyland planned with some young friends. Both Johnny and John can't do it then, either. At least we have nice phone talks, which is important for keeping our bonds. My shoulder is healed, and I'm left edgy for desert solitude therapy, but without the usual cure. The wife will be out of town, so I decide to work out a shorter, different, solo adventure.

I wake at 4:00 a.m. as if I'm going to work, but instead I pack up the motorcycle and am out by 7:00, on my way to Joshua Tree National Park. It's not as far as DVNP from our place north of Phoenix, is much smaller than DVNP, and with an elevation of 3,000 to 4,000 feet, is usually free of snow in March. This should work out.

Interstate 10 across the Mojave Desert from Arizona is not ugly scenery; it is just that I've seen it fifty times. I'm also not one of those people who rides a motorcycle because it can go fast. The curvier old two-lane routes to the north are slower but have some fair-to-great scenery. That plus the solitude and adventure of being on the motorcycle are already having a positive effect.

A bit east of Joshua Tree National Park, I stop along a fence and formerly stately tree next to the highway where thousands of discarded shoes are hung. I don't know how something like this gets started, because there is no other reason to stop there. It is weird, if perhaps not what you'd call scenic. I don't contribute my hiking boots.

The paved roads in Joshua Tree have collectively earned a spot in Reader's Digest's *The Most Scenic Drives in America*, and there are not so many roads here that you can't drive most of them in a day, if you don't make many stops. Of course, I stop a few times. I take a two-mile hike around Skull Rock and ride to Keys View overlook, which allows one to see down into the Coachella Valley to the San Jacinto Mountains. This valley is now home to half a million people.

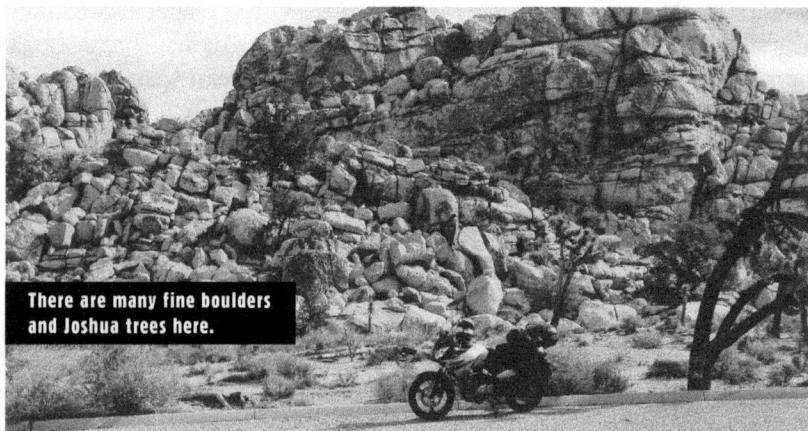

There are many fine boulders and Joshua trees here.

By midafternoon, I stop the machine in a parking lot, unload everything into a daypack, and then bungee a pad and sleeping bag to it. From here is a ten- to twelve-mile loop through Stubbe Springs, so I head out that way, figuring that I'll stop about halfway and spend the night. The trail is clearly marked and pleasant. It is not as vast and varied as DVNP, but Joshua Tree is still beautiful, with its piles of boulders and stands of stately Joshua trees. Some say that Joshua Tree is in a vast positive energy vortex, like those that supposedly enhance Sedona, Arizona. I'm not so tuned in that I can verify that, but I do feel very good here.

There is a sandy wash that the trail crosses about five or six miles in that looks good for a stop. I've seen no other humans in the last four miles, so the place is vacant except for me—and a lot of rodents, from the looks of the burrows. I get the bedding set up in the soft sand and am hungry for one of those tasty, freeze-dried dinners in a bag. Oh, man, I forgot the butane stove! Dinner is, therefore, half a pound of trail mix. At least I have plenty of water to wash it down.

A beautiful full moon rises to the east, aligned over this dry wash. A full moon in the clear desert is wonderful, unless you are trying to sleep under it without a tent. And being a full moon, it will be bright and above me all night long. Too bad it doesn't throw any heat, because the perfectly warm day has turned chilly. I put on everything, including the motorcycle jacket and gloves, before crawling into the famously marginally effective sleeping bag that I still have not upgraded.

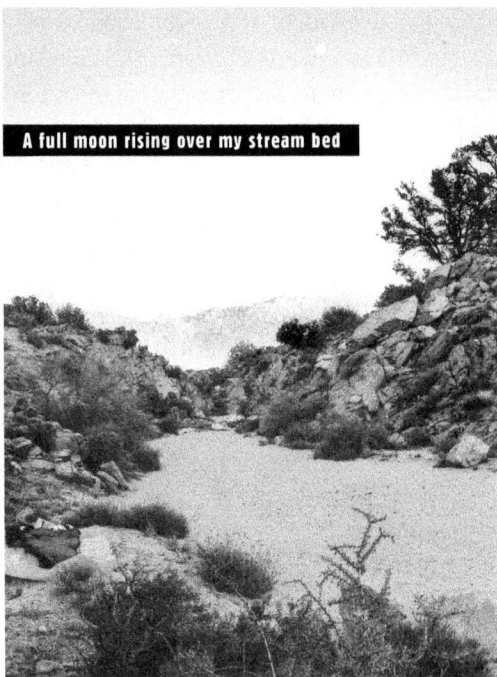

A full moon rising over my stream bed

In defense (again) of not buying an expensive and better sleeping bag, over these many years I've only been really cold in it for a few nights and have survived them by wearing my clothes to bed. For most of the nights in DVNP, we have camped in fair weather or had a cabin to hide in for the night. Every year, I'm able to rationalize that I can postpone buying a new bag because it appears that this year, I won't need it. At least most of the time I've been right. Those other nights, well, I've just been cold.

Only rarely in Death Valley does one hear a commercial jet, even distantly, apparently because it is just as remote for flight paths as it is for surface travel. Joshua Tree, however, is below many Southern California commercial flight paths, not too far from Palm Springs International Airport, and even closer to the Twentynine Palms Marine base. The Marines seem to flight train a lot at night with big helicopters, at least when they know I'm trying to sleep nearby. There is also some light pollution from the few hundred thousand residents in the Coachella Valley to the south, so stargazing is somewhat compromised by that and the full moon. Officially, Joshua Tree is an International Dark Sky Park, but DVNP is way better for stargazing.

In the morning, there is obviously nothing hot to eat (no stove) and little to pack. The weather is mild, the trail quiet and attractive, and the ride out of the park extremely pleasant. This trip does not feature a fine dinner or a warm and quiet night, but it is still good, and now I have these stories to tell. A smooth motorcycle is a wonderful companion on a slowly winding road through a national park. Breakfast at the Andreas diner in Twentynine Palms is tasty, plentiful, and hot. The ride home is quiet and scenic. It is a fine way to spend two days, hiking twelve miles and riding 610 miles.

## Hiking Lessons

1. *Remember the lesson from the first trip, where you check all of your gear before leaving.*

2. *A twenty-pound day pack, complete with the sleeping bag, barely slows you down. It's a lot easier to manage than a full trek pack with more than twice the weight.*

3. *Groomed trails are so much easier than hikes without trails.*

4. *Joshua Tree National Park is scenic, but DVNP is grander, larger, and better for our purposes.*

5. *It's probably wise that I don't go solo off trail alone, considering my history.*

6.  Given a choice, try to plan camping trips around the time of a new moon.

## Life Lessons

1.  It could have been even better with my friends.

2.  The therapeutic effects of even a two-day solo hike were helpful. Life in the raw, even for just this short time, gives me a greater appreciation for the home and wife.

3.  Don't sell the motorcycle.

4.  I'm not yet too old or worn out for this stuff. Stay in shape.

# 2018

# Racetrack Valley & The Corridor

*Are We Getting Too Old for This?*

The first thing you should know is that there is no real racetrack in DVNP. This is the name for a remote (even for Death Valley) playa (former lake bed) at 3,710' elevation. This extremely smooth, flat clay surface is about a mile wide and two miles long. It is called the Racetrack because there are many fist-sized stones scattered on the surface that leave tracks where they have slid. Until not long ago, there was no verified explanation for this phenomenon. The summers are hot and the winters are cold in Racetrack Valley, and there are, as usual in DVNP, no facilities in the one camping spot south of the Racetrack. Although the view is spectacular, spending weeks or months watching the rocks on the playa for something to happen might be a little boring.

One winter morning, some observers were there in particularly inhospitable conditions: after rain, a freezing night, and howling winds that morning. The thin frozen layer of ice on the playa broke into pieces. Some of the rocks were on ice sheets that tipped up and acted as sails. The clay here is very slippery when wet, so the wind pushed the sails and their little stone ships across the surface, leaving furrows to mark the paths. The ice melted and the water evaporated, removing all evidence. Cool.

Brad and I had discussed going to Racetrack Valley last year when the group trip fizzled. Instead, he took his sons and reported to us that the destination was terrific. We like the idea because we are getting older, and this destination may be a farther drive than we will be willing to do in future years. There are still many places in DVNP to explore that are closer. It was also encouraging that Brad had already scoped out the area, found a great camping spot near the car parking area, and tested out a cross-country day trip. In our enthusiasm, we overlooked the details about what could be, in Brad's perspective, 1) near the parking area and 2) a nice day hike. Well, if we had stayed away from the unknown or challenging, we would have missed out on most of our adventures. What the heck.

It is a bit amazing that we always arrive at our Stovepipe Wells reunion point just a few minutes apart, and seeing the guys again is wonderful. This February I'm a little tired, but I don't want to admit it to myself or the others. After breakfast, we have about an hour on paved roads going north before getting to Ubehebe Crater, which is the remainder of a relatively recent volcanic eruption. The road southwest of here is dirt, but this won't be the first time that the Element has gotten its tires dirty. Brad has a new crew-cab Chevy pickup, and it glides down this washboard road effortlessly. The Element sounds and feels like it will disintegrate at any speed above twelve miles per hour. Since it is twenty-five miles to the Racetrack, I pull over. Rather than take two hours to drive this stretch, we pile all of my stuff into Brad's truck and leave the Element. The Chevy can easily travel at thirty miles per hours or more, and now we are all together.

The road climbs as high as 4,910' elevation, and the scenery is easy to appreciate at this modest velocity. There is a Joshua tree forest here that would do justice to Joshua Tree National Park. Joshua trees only exist within a limited elevation range, determined by where their pollinating moths can live. It is interesting to drive through this isolated forest of unique flora that has whatever it takes to thrive.

About twenty miles along, we come to Teakettle Junction. This is where Racetrack Valley Road is joined by another dirt road, even more primitive. The spot would have no other significance except that the signpost here, initially decorated with a single teapot, now has innumerable colorful teakettles on and around it. It is required to take pictures here. In the photos, we can read Johnny's shirt. He is a martial arts expert, and his shirt reads, "Surely not *everybody* was Kung Fu fighting."

The Racetrack is only five miles further, and we park near there at a trailhead that goes to the west up to Ubehebe Peak. To the east of here is a rocky island on the eerily smooth Racetrack. This granite outcrop about a quarter mile out in the playa is called the Grandstand and is a natural draw for inquisitive souls. The weather is mild, so we just start walking out. It is amazing how you can lose a sense of distance and feel so utterly vulnerable on this blank surface, even just walking out to the Grandstand. This outcrop and its sparse vegetation feel much more familiar and cozier to climb around. Eventually we venture to wander more on the playa, looking for moving rocks. Without having to search too long on the otherwise featureless surface, we find some. Considering that these rough cobbles originated from the mountains on the south bank over a mile away, they have had a good long slide. The only downer in our playa wandering is that some fool has driven their vehicle out here, marring its surface. We take consolation in knowing that enough time and rain should smooth over those tire tracks.

Racetrack Valley Road dead-ends at the abandoned Homestake copper mine, less than three miles further. A few other vehicles have made it to the Racetrack with us; a couple are adventure-style motorcycles like mine, and another is the most rugged camper I have ever seen. When we get back to our truck, Brad instructs us that we are going to camp partway up the trail to Ubehebe Peak. That is good because we aren't supposed to camp down here, and he says that the view up the trail is spectacular. Just having a trail is a positive condition that we have rarely experienced in DVNP. It's not so good that the spot Brad has in mind is three-quarters of a mile away

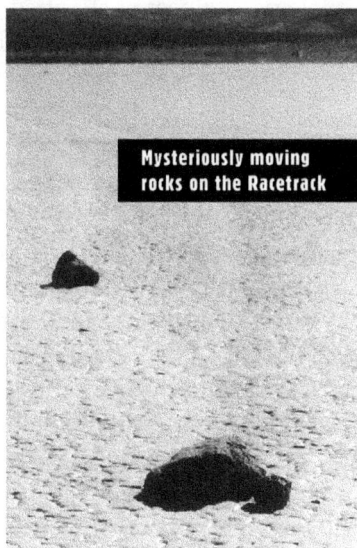

Mysteriously moving rocks on the Racetrack

and nearly 500 feet higher in elevation. Because this trip was to feature "car camping," I've brought thick cushions, camp chairs, a tent, and a telescope. My burro-like friends and I lug everything except the telescope in one trip. Again, I'm feeling a little tired and so am unwilling to make a second trip for the telescope.

This moderate burst of climbing exercise on a steep and rocky trail feels OK to me, but is slow going for Johnny, whose knees keep getting worse. We ascend to a gently rounded knoll about the size of a suburban house property. Past here, the trail continues its steep path to Ubehebe Peak, which sits hard against us to the west and will soon shade this area. In every other direction is a panoramic view of the Racetrack, the valley that cradles it, and the Cottonwood Mountains a few miles to the east that define this valley. It is probably the most magnificently scenic campsite that we have ever had. We congratulate Brad on his excellent choice. From now until we leave the site in two days, we will encounter nobody else.

Although still daylight, at about 4,200 feet up and in the shade of 5,678-foot Ubehebe Peak, it is already getting cool. We claim and modestly smooth our places to sleep. I need a little more room, as I've brought my small tent. As much as I love stargazing, I've never invested in that premium sleeping bag, and the cheap 35-year-old tent is my extra protective layer against the wind and cold that I thought might accompany this sleepover at a bit of elevation. For every 1,000 feet of elevation gain, the temperature drops, on average, 4.2 degrees Fahrenheit, so our site is now 17 degrees cooler than the valley floor—plus the wind chill.

The night is cold, but the extra thick pads help a lot. Even in the tent, I wear thermal underwear and a jacket to sleep in, and that keeps me toasty. We arise before the sun and I get some excellent scenery photos. The other three guys hugging their cups of tea in down jackets and watch caps make a defining statement about the weather.

This next thing is going to sound strange to most, but here goes. If you have to have your morning bowel movement in nature, leaning back against a giant boulder with a view of this valley makes an otherwise always-forgotten activity memorable. It beats staring at the bathroom door.

Knowing we have a Brad-designed hike ahead of us, John and I fill our day packs and get ready to descend to the truck. Johnny will stay in camp to savor the view and read. The canvas camp chairs I brought were primarily with his comfort in mind.

The Ubehebe Mine turnoff is only three miles north on Racetrack Valley Road. There is a lot to look into at this old mining site, but Brad has promised us a long hike, so we mostly walk on by. We'll investigate more if we have time when we return.

We ascend the trailless canyon, both John and I completely unaware of where we are but trusting Brad because he was here only a year ago. We come to an inches-wide parapet that ascends along an otherwise sheer face, which gets us about thirty feet above the canyon floor. This cling-to-the-wall scoot on loose rock is a bit nerve-wracking because OSHA-compliant railing still has not come to DVNP. John is visibly and understandably nervous. Maybe I'm hiding my fear. Maybe not.

A short while later, Brad climbs a rather intimidating twenty-foot fall without his backpack. Glad for two working shoulders, I throw our three packs and hiking sticks up to him, even though the climb looks like one Doogie or I could fall from. Brad wraps a rope around a big boulder at the top, descends via the rope, and proceeds to fit John and instruct us in rope-assisted climbing. We had no idea that BJ had brought ropes and intended to use them on, I mean *for*, us. John and I are a little advanced in years to be learning a new athletic skill like this. John gamely keeps trying despite some discouraging failures. After several tries with Brad at the top and me below, he gets up. As John would say, "It wasn't pretty." I've had a bit of bouldering experience and practice at climbing walls. Now with two functional shoulders and the rope, I succeed.

I think it is at this point that John and I ask if this is the way we are returning. Brad says no, it is a loop. We realize that does not necessarily mean it will be easier on the way back, but it will be different! We also now have little warning lights in our brains telling us that Brad did this last year with young adults and teenagers, not senior citizens. We had conveniently forgotten that fact until now.

The next obstacle should be fun, but I manage to botch it. We have gone as high as we'll be going and now get to slide on our butts down a polished dolomite fall that is not too scary-steep or high. In my exuberance, I hit my tailbone. It's a pain I'd like to do without, but it passes and does not prevent me from walking.

The Corridor

It is admittedly a beautiful hike, albeit challenging, and the best is yet to come. After a bit over three miles of travel, we descend down boulders into the upper end of the Corridor. This slot canyon is about thirty feet wide and has walls seventy feet high, essentially vertical, and virtually straight for almost a mile. Brad has led us to a magnificent place like no other. We walk on the sand down to the mouth of the canyon and have lunch. We all enjoy the view of the valley below as we share food. We miss Johnny, who always has interesting chow and good conversation.

Brad uses maps to confirm how to make a loop out of this hike, more or less copying last year. We descend to the large wash along the base of these mountains and walk north up it, looking to the east for a likely way to climb over the ridge and get back to the little canyon where Ubehebe Mine and the truck are. The ridge looks awfully high from where we are. John and I are getting a little tired, and we become inquisitive about the walk back, figuring that we are only about halfway. Brad shares his map with us.

Topographic maps define features with lines of equal elevation, in this case eighty feet apart. There are a lot of lines between us and the top of this ridge, and I would like to cross as few of those topo lines as possible. Brad finds the intersecting wash that he believes we should ascend to get us over the ridge line, so we take it. My low energy level, which seemed a little suspect yesterday, is again making itself felt, but I figure it won't help to complain. John is also slowing down, but he never, ever complains. Part of the way up we study the map some more, looking for the easiest possible route. I suggest a direction that takes us around the peak in front of us, trekking a contour to the other side. The troupe last year did not have to do that, but they were either four decades younger or named Brad.

We march on. The crest is within sight, but our chosen path on the side of the peak is at an angle to our direction of travel and composed of loose rocks. This course will save climbing and distance, so we continue. I am trying to lead, but I am tired. I lose my footing, and despite the hiking poles, I fall straight back onto my butt, with a rock stopping the drop by centering itself on my tailbone. I roll onto my side and lie still, moaning. Two injuries to the same spot within hours. This feels like trying to learn how to snowboard, except we could not be in a more remote place. Again, Ken has broken himself and potentially destroyed the adventure.

Brad and John are concerned. Fortunately, after several minutes the pain subsides some and we find the ibuprofen. Apparently, at this level of injury, a damaged tailbone mostly just makes sitting painful, while walking is still

OK. I vow to not push so hard out here where no help is available and to stop when I may be too tired to keep myself from falling. Without a functional body, I won't get back as planned. It is becoming clear to this slow learner that whatever my capability was before, it currently isn't there.

After our unintended but useful rest break, we ascend the rest of the way to the top. Crossing over the ridge is comically easy. When we see the gentle grade ahead, John gives Brad a thankful, nervous hug. The descent down the east side is practically a stroll, with no scary falls or unstable descents in the next two or three miles. It was wise of Brad to decide on this direction for the loop, as those earlier obstacles would have been even more of a problem with fatigue added in. We have a little energy left when we get to the truck—or maybe it is adrenaline because we are returning mostly intact. It is not too late to look around this abandoned copper mine for a bit.

We climb into the truck, not getting too relaxed yet, knowing we have that almost mile-long climb back to camp. Having a trail, though, certainly makes it easier, and we surge up. The campsite is already in shadow, and Johnny cheerfully greets us. There were high winds here today, as opposed to nearly still conditions where we had hiked only a few miles away. Johnny

Not your average campsite

had thoughtfully weighed down everyone's equipment with boulders and put an especially large number of them in my tent. If he hadn't been here, the tent and all of our stuff would have blown way, way down the mountain slope. What a nice guy.

I push through changing clothes and eat dinner in a rush. I can't sit comfortably and am tired and sore, so I retire apologetically just as it gets dark. I can hear the other men conversing for a while, but then the wind drowns out all other sounds for the rest of the night.

The morning dawns, quiet and beautiful. It would be great to take a half day to climb Ubehebe Peak on this real trail, but we all have long drives ahead, especially me. We busy ourselves packing everything, again like miners' burros. Brad sets the pace down the trail, of course. It is not windy now and the temperature is in the 60s—darned pleasant for a hike.

The drive north on Racetrack Valley Road is beautiful and the conversation is engaging, as always. When we get to the Element there is some sorting and repacking, and the wind is picking up. We drive together another mile or two to Ubehebe Crater where we expect to hike, but the breeze has turned into a gale up here. We hug goodbye instead and pile into our steel and glass cocoons, thankful to accept the comforts of modern life. Brad drives faster than me, so they gradually pull away and finally out of sight on Death Valley Road. At Highway 190, they will turn west, and I'll go east. It is 10:30 a.m. and I have almost 400 miles left.

I'm fatigued more than I've been on any other trip, and on the way out of DVNP I lose my attention and two wheels of the car drift off the road. Fortunately, the shoulder is forgiving here, and I can correct the error with no harm done. I decide to drink coffee and must force myself to be especially diligent for this day's drive. My tail bone hurts, so I take ibuprofen and do my best to cushion it and shift around. I get home a little while after dark. My friends arrive home without incident.

## Hiking Lessons

1.  Trust Brad to set up an interesting adventure.

2.  Trust Brad to set up a challenging adventure.

3.  Climbing with ropes is not magically easy. It still requires strength and skill.

4.  Walking a contour on a steep slope with no trail is about as hard as

*just going up the darn slope. Maybe it is less stable, and you should just go up the slope.*

5. *Pay attention to your current energy level more than to some historical perspective of what used to be possible.*

6. *I believe that between Johnny's knees, John's intelligent nervousness in situations where a fall could maim him, and my declining strength, we have reached a point where the type of adventure we take will have to be dialed back for all of us to participate.*

## Life Lessons

1. *We may have figured out why there are not a lot of really old mountain climbers.*

2. *There is something happening that makes me tire more easily than before.*

3. *Going to the Racetrack may have been a smart do-it-while-you-can trip. "Do it while you can" is not a bad motto to avoid some regrets.*

4. *Also be cautious about do-it-even-if-you-can't to avoid possible regrets.*

# 2019

# Ventures From Stovepipe Wells

*Share the Wonders While We Can*

After the 2018 hike, each new month feels like a tick towards the ending of a phase.

**March:** Tail bone hurts. The doctor says that recovery can take a year or more. Able to walk, but not pushing it more than a few miles. Write a letter to my three amigos saying that I think we need to rethink our type of annual adventures.

**April:** Need naps more often.

**May:** Less energy, needing even longer naps. No big walks or other significant exercise.

**June:** Diagnosed with diabetes and begin meds. Too tired to work after June 18 and also have a sore lower back. Fly with Voni to Florida for a week's vacation. Can only walk one to two miles, if at all, and need one or two long naps each day. Voni stays in Florida because her father has terminal Parkinson's disease.

**July:** My blood work comes back negative for cancer, vitamin deficiencies, or other diagnosable diseases. Able to work only a few hours per day.

Begin antibiotics. Begin counseling and journaling. Voni's father dies. Poor family support for her mom causes great stress.

**August:** Primary care doctor has no medical answer. The urologist is of no help. The endocrinologist says that my diabetes is under control. The dietician says I'm doing well but can improve. I have tinnitus now. Only working about four hours a day, fueled by caffeine or adrenaline when there is an urgent task. Often must sleep in the car before leaving work in order to drive home safely.

**September:** Still unable to work longer than four hours a day. Journaling and counseling seem to have dealt with personal issues. Doctor does not think I have had mini-strokes, mold allergy, or any other documentable illness. May have a full-body inflammation causing insulin resistance and fatigue. I'm in a continuous daze. The doctor agrees with me that if after three months I haven't gotten better while working, there may be no choice but to retire.

**October:** Can barely make it up one story of stairs when walking back to the car after work each day. Tell bosses I will retire at the end of the month. Do so.

After a reworking of our house, Voni's mother flies back to live with us in January. Voni organized all of her mom's belongings and I have gained enough strength to drive the moving van from Florida to Arizona, towing Mom's car. Voni has been working way too hard for a disabled person, and she has a couple of fainting episodes. The paramedics and the hospital doctors have no helpful diagnoses, but charge us anyway, of course. Her mother also collapses a couple of times but does not pass out. All we can do is make sure that nobody is alone. I'm recovered enough to drive all day or unload and move furniture but know that it is partially due to adrenaline and necessity, similar to Voni's heroic work with her mother. I'm not close to my strength of previous years.

Honest talks with Johnny and John determine that their lives this year are in no less crisis, and their physical conditions have also declined. Brad has a very extensive route planned with a younger group. I know it would be foolish to attempt to keep up with them now. Is this what getting old is like? We can't seem to put together a group hike this year, but I hope this is not the end of our adventures.

Also in this year, my late wife's mother, still close to us, is experiencing a fast health decline, causing distress. My father is having trouble with sight, memory, coordination, and thought organization, so he can't drive out of his community and probably shouldn't drive at all. A few years ago, he dropped his motorcycle and finally, regretfully, sold it. He is holding his ground against his children and wife about going into a retirement community. This is clearly where my siblings and I inherited our stubborn independence.

Hang on—maybe I can still create a DVNP experience this year for the benefit of many. Dad agrees for me to pick him up and go overnight to Death Valley. He remembers the past vividly, including his motorcycle trips to DVNP in the 1970s with his friend Ron. Back then he rode a full-dress Honda 750, fitted with accessory oil coolers. Dad was taking temperature readings for the oil cooler manufacturer's field testing. That testing including riding in Death Valley in the summer, and the corporate sponsorship made his ride essentially free. He'd love to return, even if it means riding in a car. His wife, my stepmother, can use the break to visit with her daughters. Win-win-win.

Even better, my brothers Dan and Ed agree to overnight in Ridgecrest, a hundred miles from DVNP, and meet us on the morning that Dad and I drive up. Both of these brothers live about 300 miles from Ridgecrest, but from different directions. DVNP is fortuitously a roughly equidistant one-day drive for all of us. After Voni says, "You will NOT make your father sleep on the ground," I am able to secure the last two available rooms in the Stovepipe Inn. We are all on board, and we three younger senior citizens will bring our mountain bikes. Dan manages a bike shop and rides daily, still sometimes competitively. Ed is a motorcycle mechanic and former desert motorcycle and downhill mountain bike racer. They are one and two years younger than me. There is no question that I will be the slowest bike rider of this threesome.

On a Saturday, I drive the 320 miles to Dad and Mom's place to spend the night. Dad and I will get up at about 5:00 a.m. and drive to DVNP. When I rise, Dad is already dressed and ready to go. He is so excited and nervous that he has been up since midnight, and Mom has been sitting quietly with him at the dining room table for hours. Dad gets more anxious these days. I act calm and efficient, hopefully assuaging their concerns that this might be too much adventure for him—and me, for that matter. We leave by 6:00 a.m.

It is 110 miles to Ridgecrest, and Sunday dawn traffic leaving Los Angeles is as light as it can ever be. Daybreak is my favorite time of day, and even the Cajon Pass north on the I-15 is enjoyably scenic in these conditions. I've brought along a handful of CDs so that Dad can pick the music he'd like. We both prefer the same era of rock and roll. We are also synchronized in that we have to stop more often these days to find a restroom.

Dad knows that Dan will meet us in Ridgecrest at a motel, but when we roll into the parking lot it is Ed that he sees standing in front of us. We had kept Ed's attendance a secret, and that stuns Dad into being speechless—not an easy thing to do to Fred. After a snack in the breakfast bar, we head out with Dan and Ed driving Ed's truck. We'll switch off, ferrying Dad in either my vehicle or Ed's, so that he will be able to visit more with everyone. Entering DVNP with the usual stunning vista impresses everyone.

After a real breakfast at Stovepipe Inn, we walk over to the ranger's station. My plan is to take the dirt road loop up to and then down the one-way Titus Canyon road, stopping for views and petroglyphs. Titus Canyon has miles of impressive narrows and was drivable by the Element and Brad's rental sedan a few years ago. It would be an awesome ten-mile mountain bike descent. The next morning, I plan for us to drive up the two-mile dirt road to Mosaic Canyon and hike the narrows there. The ranger informs me that the upper end of Titus Canyon and the road to Mosaic Canyon are both closed due to flood damage. Maybe it was the same rain that transformed Marble Canyon two years ago. I fake confidence and assure the family that I'll figure out some other adventures suitable for us.

I remember the year that we drove up to a place called Hole-in-the-Wall on a dirt road and recall that it was quite scenic and not too steep. The ranger says that Hole-In-The-Wall road starts near the Twenty Mule Team Canyon Road, which is smooth dirt and one way. He recommends that we bicycle it in reverse. He also says that the dirt road going up to the base of Titus Canyon is still open, and we can park there to take a walk up the canyon for a way. Being flexible and not acting hopeless has gotten my regular hiking group out of many situations, and that positive attitude now makes it possible to establish a fun routine for this group as well. A recheck of the map and off we go.

At the base of the Hole-in-the-Wall road, we leave the truck and add Ed's bike to the back of the Element, and Dan powers up the road on his mountain bike. The Element is over its recommended net carrying capacity now, which has never stopped me before but does slow us down while climbing a rough gravel road. Even uphill, Dan is quite a bit faster than us on his bicycle. This surprises nobody.

Dad finds this off-highway travel exciting. I let him drive for a half mile or so, and he doesn't get us stuck. When we get to a deep wash, I ask to take back the wheel, preferring to be the one who either grinds the undercarriage or gets us stuck. Grind we do, but we manage to keep making progress.

After just a few miles, we've lost sight of Dan and there are now alternate routes branching out. I should have thought to have him wait at any junctions. Not wanting to miss him if we take a different path, I park within view of the Hole-in-the-Wall. Dad used to have the loudest whistle on the planet, which us Rocklings could hear two blocks away and told us that it was time to hustle home for dinner. Dad tries to whistle for Dan, but it comes out as a wheeze. He is visibly disappointed, as are Ed and I. Ah, well, the whistle worked before, when it was really essential.

Regardless, it doesn't take long for Dan to come storming down the road to meet us. It is quiet and beautiful here, so we enjoy these conditions for a bit. Ed and I get into our cycling clothing and take our bikes off the back of the car, where Dan straps on his bike. Dan used to have an Element, as have two other members of our family, so there is no question about his handling it down the grade. The car rides a little lighter now, and downhill is always easier because you can roll through the loose stuff, rather than trying to power up it. Ed and I will ride down this road and then take the Twenty Mule Team Canyon Road, meeting Dad and Dan at the end of it. Away!

I remember well a lesson from many years ago that says it is dangerously stupid to try and keep up with Ed on a downhill mountain bike ride. He always has better equipment but would still be able to leave me in the dust even if his tires were mostly flat. Today, fortunately, Ed would rather ride with me. Ed and Dan both have elite dual-suspension bikes, while mine is a hard tail, meaning no rear suspension. Ed says later that watching the back of my bike bounce around kept him from getting too close, thinking that I might crash at any time. Being excited and energized, I go as fast as I can, only scaring myself a few times when the front tire washes out and threatens to pitch me off. Ed says he noticed that as well. What an exciting downhill—not too steep, but still plenty fast. It's also a plus that I don't wipe out.

Dan, Ken, and Ed Rock on their mechanical steeds

Next, we pedal the mile up the paved highway to the Twenty Mule Team Canyon Road, where we turn in. Normally I'd never ride the wrong way on a one-way road, but the ranger said it was OK. This two-mile-long dirt road has a smooth surface that is occasionally dusted with loose sand. That's not a great combination for two-wheeled cornering. So as not to lose traction, Ed and I contain our enthusiasm on the steep downhills. These two miles seem longer because the road undulates and carves around the hills, and the climbs require first gear, good for only three miles per hour. Insofar as climbing on a bicycle, today Ed and I are at about the same fitness level, or at least he lets me think so. The hills are starkly barren, eroded badlands—the ranger made an outstanding recommendation for this road. Would it be at least as beautiful going the proper direction? Yeah, probably. Dan and Dad are waiting for us at the end of the road. Dad says that Dan drives the Element much faster than me on a gravel road. A lot of people, especially those in my family, do things better than me, so I simply swallow the assessment.

When we get back to Ed's truck, I have another idea. Dan can ride his bike to Furnace Creek, which is over 1,000 feet lower in elevation. It doesn't take him any time to say yes. A mountain bike is not the fastest type of bike on a road, but Dan has a lot of aerodynamic experience from road and track bicycles, so he makes the best of it. Because the road is not really steep or winding, we are faster in the motor vehicles, but don't have to wait more than ten minutes before Dan arrives.

It is early afternoon, so we take a break to eat some food that we've brought. Having a few hours of daylight left, we drive north about thirty miles and then drive two and a half miles up an alluvial fan on a fairly smooth dirt road to the mouth of Titus Canyon. There is a good parking lot with numerous other cars and, amazingly, restrooms. The canyon mouth is where the narrows are, and it beckons us.

I've brought an extra pair of hiking boots and poles for my dad. It is a bittersweet privilege to lace up your parent's boots because they can no longer do that. Dad doesn't seem terribly embarrassed, excited as he is to be here with his three sons. That's great. We walk up the gravel that is the road. The narrows are between twenty and sixty feet wide, which means that the entire floor is the stream bed when it rains a lot. That also means that the entire width of the narrows is the road. Due to the closure, there are no vehicles coming down the canyon, so we can wander around as we please.

Athletes Ed and Dan don't require hiking boots or poles to comfortably walk the narrows. I use both, for my own safety but also to provide an example for Dad. This is a man who was extremely coordinated, working on and riding scooters and motorcycles for most of his adult life. At age eighty-six, though, mastering walking sticks as I instruct him is not working. In slow going, you can swing your hands (like in a regular walk) while planting the sticks. The poles provide useful stability for Dad, but he walks like a camel, with both right limbs and both left limbs moving together. Well, it works for camels, who have evolved to a life of walking in sand, so maybe I'm the one who doesn't do it right.

A stroll in the Titus Canyon narrows

Dad sees shapes in the cliffs, as if gazing at clouds. Very interesting. Ed likes to pick up little rocks, examine, and then throw them. That is such *Ed* behavior. The sheer canyon faces, perfect weather, and silence are intoxicating. On a climbable wall slope, we stage a photo for Dad similar to a picture that he took of us almost sixty years ago on a low, massive oak tree branch, where we are huddled behind each other as if riding a toboggan. This hour with the four of us walking in the Titus Canyon narrows is a simple, yet peak experience—the type that marks our lives as enjoyable and worth remembering. The family bond is being reinforced.

Narrows are shady more often than sunlit, but I sense that the sun is descending. We turn around and in fifteen minutes the canyon mouth becomes visible, opening to a vast vista of Death Valley as we cross the narrow's threshold. Our spirits are high and the sun is low.

It is twilight as we check into our rooms. We quickly shower and get ready for the dining room, anxious for a good meal. We are not disappointed, and the bonding is subtle, but warm and comfortable. After dinner there is a bit of a walk back to our rooms in the dry and pleasant evening.

Dan goes straight to bed, but Ed brings his guitar over to the room I'm sharing with Dad. Dad played guitar until about fifteen years ago. His technique was enthusiastic, and he had several songs memorized. Dad sang pretty well—and especially loud. I've also picked up the guitar and play better than he did but am not good at memorizing songs (or anything else) and I don't sing as well as he did. Or nearly as loud. Siblings Rick and Angela also play the instrument. Rick is primarily a drummer yet might play guitar the best. Ed is currently playing in a band and has worked to memorize some songs. Ed is also the best singer by far and the least inhibited, having inherited that aspect from Dad. Ed performs great music for us, including a Garth Brooks classic, while Dad beats time on the nightstand and partially remembers some lyrics.

Dad has always beat time to music, whether it is on a beer can, table, or steering wheel. I find out during this trip that he played drums and a horn in high school. Huh—it took me this long to learn that information. We carry on until a little past 10:00 p.m., when I suggest we go to bed before the curfew police shut us down or the neighbors start banging on the walls. It is another marvelous family experience.

The next day dawns a typical DVNP winter morning, with comfortable, dry, clear weather. We have breakfast in the only (and good) restaurant here, pack up, and go down the road for one last little adventure. Just a short drive from Stovepipe Wells, there are sand dunes right next to the road. There is a paved parking lot and restrooms, as this is a popular and accessible landmark. I lace up Dad's boots and we walk out into the dunes. This is a great place for photos, with the backdrop of the Panamint Mountains. We see the tracks of lizards and mice that live under the clumps of brush that manage to survive here. We do what other people our age might consider frolicking until the adult voices in our heads tell us it is time to get going. We all have significant drives home and none of us is young enough to look forward to that. We hug goodbye, then my siblings head west, while Dad and I head east.

Usually, I go through a car wash on the way home from DVNP, as the car is always deep with dust. I do that in Henderson, Nevada, where Dad needs a long time in the restroom. That works out OK. We enter Arizona, and the drive down Highway 93 across the open desert is made even better with rock and roll selected by Dad, often accompanied by his rapping on the dashboard. We stop at a lone restaurant, miles from anywhere, as I like to do. The atmosphere of local ranchers and travelers is interesting, and the food is fine and affordable. About fifty miles from home in the town of Wickenburg, we make a stop at McDonalds for the restroom, drinks, and calories. Across the highway are tall eucalyptus trees with a large flock of turkey vultures settling in for the night. It has been my observation that turkey vultures are silent but somehow still communicate and have a communal bond, as their clans always gather in the same trees to spend the nights. I've seen turkey vulture gathering trees like this in Thousand Oaks, California, and Ely, Nevada. If you can get past the fact that they are giant ugly black birds that feed exclusively on rotting flesh, it's pretty cool how they congregate.

Our drive is over 400 miles but very pleasant, and we get to my house in Arizona at dusk. After a day here, I'll drive Dad home to California.

## Hiking Lessons

1. *Ask a ranger before you decide to go anywhere in DVNP.*

2. *There seems to be more than one technique to using hiking poles.*

3. *DVNP adventures can include mountain bikes, at least with the Rock clan.*

4. *OK, everyone would not enjoy DVNP in the way that my usual hiking group addresses it. Still, there are plenty of other adventures here that are appreciated by more conventional people—if you can call my family that.*

5. *I'm not saying it isn't exciting when it happens, but activities don't have to get you lost or in fear to be rewarding.*

6. *Being flexible and positive gives you adventure options.*

## Life Lessons

1. *Although I missed my usual hiking partners, this year's short adventure added at least equal value to the lives of four people, especially my father. It was meant to be.*

2.  I'll never play guitar or sing as well as Ed, but that doesn't make my efforts worthless.

3.  I'll never ride a bicycle as powerfully as Dan, that doesn't mean I should stop riding.

4.  Efforts to keep our independent and far-flung family bonded are rewarding.

5.  Appreciate parents while you can. Next year it may not be possible to do some things.

6.  Being flexible and positive gives you adventure options.

# 2020

# Seeing Things That Regular Folks Might

*Very Alone, Even for DVNP*

Being anxious to keep the tradition alive, I send out a proposed DVNP itinerary with my Christmas cards to each hiking friend. Sensing the advance of Father Time, this year I suggest no cross-country routes and shorter hikes, with some visits to places that are popular to most visitors, but that we have never seen. After the New Year, I follow up with proposed dates. Being retired, I am flexible except that my mother-in-law's health and need for attention may preclude my participation. She is in Texas and has just been diagnosed with cancer, and treatment is urgently needed. The coronavirus epidemic, COVID-19, hasn't been acknowledged yet.

Coordination with my hiking friends isn't going much smoother. In the end, BJ plans a trip during spring break with his young entourage. The scale of that adventure and timing don't work for John and Johnny, who also have job and family health obligations. Voni and I end up sacrificing our holiday time and much of February for her mom's physical and emotional needs. The family dynamics have degraded in the stress, or perhaps it is just that some of the previously hidden problems are being revealed.

In mid-March, Voni flies home from Texas to rest and I drive the van back. At this time, our nation finally admits that COVID-19 is something that might be serious. On the drive home, I get laryngitis and cold symptoms with some weakness. That's not consistent with COVID-19 symptoms, but it's still suspicious and bad. For this reason, the wife vacates our home to stay at a friend's house before I get home. She is already lung-compromised, and we don't want to risk her getting seriously ill. The country shuts down.

After a week of unpacking, paying bills, cleaning house, doing taxes, etc., I'm still sounding bad, but I have a bit more strength and less congestion. Voni is starting to tire of being away from home. On March 21, two days after spring begins, I leave the house for DVNP so that Voni can return home. None of the other guys can accommodate my last-minute dash, which might be just as well, considering my still somewhat marginal health and the virus scare.

I figure that DVNP is a fine place to socially distance myself and hopefully continue to improve my health. It's also a desperate grasp at keeping the DVNP tradition intact in some fashion.

The drive out is spooky. There are very few semitrucks on the highway and car traffic is scarce. Driving through Las Vegas on a Saturday evening is usually congested, but today I can use the cruise control most of the time. I've never seen the roads so deserted.

Rather than deal with motels and my potentially inhospitable condition, I will camp in our van tonight. It is a small commercial van that I've outfitted with a toilet, along with a curtain, shelves, a short bench seat, and some other accessories. The idea was to make it possible for Voni and her mom to travel, but when I stop for the night at 12:00 a.m., this little setup is perfect for one somewhat sick isolationist. It occurs to me that after a lifetime of trying to improve the world in some meaningful way through my profession, my most significant contribution might be the configuration of a toilet in a vehicle that easily fits in the garage. It is substantially less conspicuous than hauling a port-a-potty on a trailer and gets twenty-eight to thirty-two miles per gallon on this trip, driving easy.

I'm near DVNP when I pull over. On a moonless night in Death Valley, you see an array of stars hardly matched anywhere else. That is true tonight. By the way, even in this isolated location, the southeast horizon has a smudge of light pollution from Las Vegas, one hundred or so miles away. On the southwest horizon is a smaller smudge of light from the Los Angeles metropolis, some 150 miles away.

I squirm, cough, and hack for a long time before finally falling sound asleep. In a while, I wake to a strange light and realize it is dawn. I use the toilet, munch granola, drink, and think briefly how this is easier than back-pack camping. As the sky lightens, I drive the few miles left into Death Valley. From this entry, the road to Dante's View intersects; I've never been there, so I take the turn. Usually, spring is the peak visiting time for DVNP, but not this Sunday. I see no one else on this road, and there is only one other car in the spacious parking lot at Dante's View.

This place is astounding! The view is as good as or better than anywhere I've seen. I hike a half mile up to Dante's Peak at 5,590' elevation, and the view only gets more awesome in every direction, with a colorful panoramic up and down Death Valley and across to Telescope Peak, some twenty miles to the west. Up here, along the trail that traces the crest of the Black Mountains, are the upper access points to Hades Canyon and Bad Canyon, both aptly named. Those canyons drop over a mile down to Badwater, at -282' elevation. Badwater is visible only two and a half miles away, which means that the descent is steeper than the south rim of the Grand Canyon. Even Digonnet hasn't taken the full length, and he makes the trip sound dangerous and impossible. If someone's life depended on me making the descent, I'd sooner jump off with a hang glider.

**Badwater viewed from the crest of the Black Mountains**

As it is, I'm quite content to just enjoy the view and walk back the groomed trail to the parking lot. That's enough adventure for me at this location. My spirits are suddenly high, and I feel perfectly healthy. This trip currently feels smart and medicinal.

Driving down to Furnace Creek and the visitor center, I find that they are all closed due to the coronavirus. All of the campgrounds are also closed. The few people I see in the parking lot look dazed. "What do we do now?" seems to be their condition. It probably doesn't faze me as much because my team doesn't traditionally use these places. The solitude in the visitor center lot is eerie, though, because I know what this situation represents.

My next stop is Golden Canyon, another popular spot that we've never been to. It feels like perfect timing to visit these types of places now, without the usual crowds. It is also synchronized with my lowered level of ambition and ability, which is now probably closer to that of most visitors.

Golden Canyon, the sign says, was one of the most popular tourist stops in decades past because it is close to Badwater Road and the park service had paved the entire narrow canyon for motor vehicle access. As with every other narrow canyon in DVNP, a flash flood washed out all but a few vestigial pieces of the pavement along with whatever else had been built there. Wow, even the old park service had to learn that lesson. Now only hikers enter.

It is a pleasant walk up for one and a half miles, eventually threading past some large chock stones that can be clambered under or over at the narrow upper end of the canyon. Almost all of the path is smooth, hard sand and not steep. I'm beginning to appreciate this hiking on established trails, smoothed by thousands of previous feet, almost none of which are currently here. The narrows and canyon are not dramatic by DVNP standards, but they are certainly a lot easier to access than most of the ones from our past.

The palette of colored rocks on Artist's Drive

All is good. The next attraction as I head south is the Artist's Drive. It's a nine-mile one-way loop with a hillside collage of marvelously colored rocks at the halfway point. This place is another cool site that I'd never seen because all of our previous time and energy had been dedicated to more epic adventures. As with Golden Canyon, there is even an outhouse here, and the road is paved the whole way. This is practically decadent—there has not been any hardship in this adventure. Funny how so far today I've seen three things that are on the visitor guide that everyone gets as they enter the park. During most trips we spend days going to places that are not even mentioned. It's a much different perspective that I'm getting this year.

Things are about to change, because the next activity I'd proposed to the other hikers was to hike up Willow Creek Canyon to the first falls, less than two and a half miles from Badwater Road. At this point I might have better assessed my health, which is acceptable at the moment but still weaker than usual. In my proposal, we'd hike up with packs and spend the night. At least I now think that hiking with a full pack for the night might not be smart, considering that most of the weight would be pharmaceuticals and facial tissue. Anyway, it shouldn't be too tough, as Digonnet calls this a pleasant half-day walk up an alluvial fan and wash, and it is only 2:00 p.m., right?

Maybe it is the excitement of being here or the mild delirium of my illness, but I should have read that description by Michel more carefully. I should also know that any trailless walk up an alluvial fan and wash is not going to be "moderate," and a half-day hike for Digonnet could be more like a death march for an elderly semi-sick Ken.

Just finding the canyon is a challenge for me. For the record, there are now mile markers, so it works to just stop at Mile 30 and look east to the biggest alluvial fan in sight. I shoulder a day pack and, of course, take walking sticks and boots; there is no trail, and I've learned that lesson. The wildflowers are in bloom. There are scattered clouds, and the weather is pleasant. The forecast that I checked a couple of days ago predicts no rain in Death Valley for this week.

The scenery is great—at least what I can see from looking down. There are many lizards, giant orange and black beetles, and a beautiful array of rocks that I have to study with every step so that I don't break a leg. Today I must be particularly careful, as there are no buddies to rescue me and all of the rangers are sequestered, staying away from sick people. There wasn't even a way to register my backcountry intentions, as we usually do.

Digonnet writes that the narrows ahead are formed from diorite, a black and white granite. Most of the rocks I'm walking on, my "scenery," are diorite, so I believe him. The lower canyon walls here are a brown fanglomerate, which is just a fancy name for what I'm walking on, only cemented with what was mud a few hundred million years ago. The strata are tilted to the west, so that as I walk east, I'm going into older, lower rock formations. With that observation, I reason that the fanglomerate must be resting on diorite. A hard rock such as diorite would logically form a narrows, because it is resistant to erosion.

**A beetle relaxes on a chunk of diorite.**

After two hours of trudging, my actual level of health is beginning to reveal itself. I finally walk past and on some solid diorite at the base of the canyon walls. The narrows might be just around the next bend—or maybe ten turns further from here. My fatigue and a little voice of reason in my head tells me to ditch this goal and turn around before I stumble more seriously. I'm glad that my friends aren't here for the disappointment. I guess it just wouldn't be the same if all alluvial fans had trails, and Brad certainly wouldn't want it that way.

Downhill is always faster, and I have to hold myself back to step carefully. The van is a welcomed sight from the canyon opening. After another mile of rock-negotiating, I'm there.

What is left of my original plan is to go further south on Badwater Road to the base of Scotty's Canyon and camp there. Scotty's Canyon is next to Ashford Canyon, at the south end of this Black Mountain range, about fifteen miles away. I belatedly study maps and the book text further before starting. I now vaguely remember the long, rough dirt road to the base of those canyons. Too tired and delirious to think of an alternative and knowing that all developed campgrounds are closed, I drive in that direction on Death Valley Road anyway.

Death Valley is spectacularly, panoramically gorgeous. Today I encounter another car about once every five miles. The forty-five-mile-an-hour speed limit and lack of traffic allow me to soak in the inexpressible beauty. Maybe it is partly from my compromised physical state, but it feels like a dream.

Yep, as I now more clearly recall from the 2009 adventure of ours, there is the primitive dirt road going east across from the Ashford Mill landmark, heading up to Ashford Canyon. The miners worked a gold mine in Ashford Canyon and hauled the ore down here to Ashford Mill. I stop for a minute to look up that long dirt road and can clearly recall Voni making me swear not to take her van on any dirt roads. After a thoughtful pause I turn instead into the Ashford Mill site, which is just a stone's throw from the highway. There is an outhouse, an information sign next to the ruins, two picnic tables, and a small sign that says "No Camping." After more moments of chaotic and delirious reasoning, I turn off the ignition. The sign says "No Camping," but the campgrounds are all closed. As the sun sets behind gathering clouds, this location has become the best place in this vast desert for me to park for the night.

Rehydrated freeze-dried lasagna tastes like the finest restaurant fare tonight. With my energy slightly elevated, I arrange gear and settle into the van to write about today as it gets dark. As much as the night sky was dramatic last night, tonight there is a full cloud cover, and it becomes as dark as a mine. With my headlamp off and my eyes open, I can see absolutely nothing. You could sleep with your eyes open and it would make no difference. For a city dweller, that might be scary. I'm too compromised to be anything but observant.

A handful of medications and thirty tissues later, I lie to sleep. The rain that wasn't predicted a few days ago begins to fall, and our van feels insanely comfortable. I wake at about 1:00 a.m. for another load of medication and sit up to write until the drugs take effect.

I ponder how bittersweet this trip and life are. Bitter because I'm lonely and miss both my wife and my hiking buddies. Sweet because I'm not freezing in the rain under a tarp, and I have everything I need in this steel cocoon. Bitter again because I don't know how much longer I'll be ill and isolated or how long "normal" will be suspended as this nation clumsily attempts to minimize the virus's casualty count. Sweet again because my wife is in her comfortable home and not ill with whatever has infected me. Joan Baez said it even more eloquently: "Diamonds and Rust."

It now seems that a sick man walking up a 2.8-mile dirt—no, now muddy—road in the morning to begin a hike up Scotty's Canyon for a few more miles would be stupid. I study the DVNP map again and see that Natural Bridge is further north in this range—another tourist attraction not far off Badwater Road, and I've never seen it. That seems like a smarter way for me to experience another aspect of DVNP after the sun rises.

Every day I think I'm getting better, but during a lot of nights, this one in particular, it feels like I may never be healthy again. If you've ever been simultaneously exhausted, sick, and wired, you'll understand why it takes over two hours and more than fifty tissues before I am finally able to lie down again.

In the morning, I feel tired and stupid. Should I not have walked eight miles yesterday? "Duh!" could be the correct answer. I drive to Natural Bridge, which has another outhouse and just a few cars in the lot. I rest for a bit and then as I lace my boots, a ranger pulls up, lights flashing on his truck. He says that they can't reliably service the outhouses every two hours, so they are shutting down all of these sites. Considering the paucity of visitors, that doesn't seem like a valid consideration, but there is no point in arguing. He says that the main park roads will stay open, at least for now, so I could drive around the park roads, but the usual tourist sites are closed. I can't drive this vehicle on the dirt roads, the campgrounds are closed, and I'm not healthy enough to backpack alone into some Digonnet-listed attraction. It seems that the bottom-line message is to head out already. At the moment, this situation seems more bitter than sweet.

It takes about ninety minutes to exit the park from here, south via Highway 178 to Shoshone, population thirty-one. I've never invested the extra half hour to take this route, via Salsberry Pass. Maybe the air is clearer due to most people staying home, but this route might have even better vistas than my usual Highway 190 path, which is rated as a scenic road. I drive slowly and soak it in, sensing that I should burn this all permanently into my memory. Society and my life feel apocalyptic now. If I can never return to DVNP, I want this pure beauty to bring a peaceful perspective to my life's best memories.

I send photos and text my friends about the status of DVNP. Brad texts back, "Thanks for the intel. An empty DVNP is paradise." I spend tonight in a cheap motel in Kingman, hoping that I'll be healthier tomorrow and can return home.

The next day, Voni gets sick with the same symptoms as me. It seems that giving her space wasn't enough. Did I not clean the house adequately? Did we have contact with the same person a few weeks ago? If there is a bright side, it is that her doctor believes that she has thrush or some other throat infection, which is treatable and not as life threatening as COVID-19.

Regardless, we'll still stay isolated from everyone else, at least now in the same house. She asks if this year's DVNP trip was necessary. "No...and yes," I say.

A week later, Brad phone-messages the three of us regulars with photos of his DVNP trip with his two sons and their friends. In one photo they are ascending a steep rock climb that would have been problematic for me and probably impossible for Johnny or John. Another photo shows him leaning on a locked gate. His text reads, "Yep, the typical Brad route, locked INSIDE the park, survived a night during a violent winter storm, beautiful next day." He has made more DVNP memories.

## Hiking Lessons

1. *Read Digonnet's hike descriptions carefully.*

2. *The base of an alluvial fan, lightly scattered with rocks, is fair to hike on. Climb it further and it degrades quickly. I know this well but seem to keep relearning the fact.*

3. *OK, I admit it: day hikes and car camping allow the older and somewhat infirm to still experience the great outdoors.*

4. *If you must hike when sick, maybe don't overdo it.*

5. *Somewhat in contradiction to the last lesson, maybe we want to do stuff while we can. Life and opportunities pass quickly, maybe never to return.*

## Life Lessons

1. *I probably deal with being alone better than most but will still say that social isolation is psychologically destructive. Stay in contact with those you love.*

2. *Much of life is bittersweet. To realize more sweetness, one probably has to allow and accept more bitter. So sorry.*

3. *Although I outfitted the van with the toilet for others, it turns out to be just as valuable for me, especially when travelling with compromised health.*

4. *Time will tell if this COVID-19 disaster is used as a reality check and reset for our collective thinking.*

# EPILOGUE

Age is not just a chronological function—it also feels like it's the effect of an accumulated weight of traumas, mistakes, and disappointments. The sobering reality is that once over the age of forty, we will never be physically better. Each year, the trend is toward reduced energy, strength, and drive. Whatever has been accomplished is likely as good as it gets in terms of defining you and your success, be it professional, personal, relationship focused, or adventure based. To make matters even more unsettling, the coronavirus pandemic of 2020 has disrupted many things that we thought we could rely on in our society and our relationships. At this point, I don't know what the future for the annual DVNP adventures looks like. In the last four years, we have had our traditional get-together only once. The tradition feels sick, like the country and humanity.

Looking through the photos from each year, in albums that are starting to fall apart from the earlier times, I see smiles and confidence that seem larger than those we have now. Part of the reason is probably that we don't take photos of the physical disasters that befall us—and none of the emotional disasters. It is like the Facebook chronicles, where we tout how wonderful and successful our lives are: all diamonds and no rust. Certainly, my memories tend to gloss over the crises, trying to keep a positive spin on why we keep moving forward, living. The alternative would leave me suicidal.

Our parents are now passed or disabled to various degrees. Not so long ago, they were strong and vital. I remember a headshot photo of my father in his motorcycle helmet, smiling broadly. Now when I look in the motorcycle mirror, someone similar but even older is looking back. I am aware that many of the aspects that define the aging of our parents are becoming visible in me. Certainly, there are many more days behind me than ahead. This is one of the reasons this book is being written; it is a semi-durable physical legacy for lives now in the last trimester.

In my family, there are examples of how to be gracious and satisfied with age and decreasing abilities, even if you were once world class. Sister Angela was on the Olympic indoor volleyball team and then became the number one beach volleyball player. Now she coaches college volleyball. Brother Dan was a top-ten triathlete, who now is a bicycle mechanic and still surfs almost daily. Brother Ed was a desert motorcycle racer and downhill mountain bike racer who now uses an electrically assisted mountain bike to ascend his favorite mountain. It is usually too late for us to change "if only" and "what if" aspects of the past. For those whose accomplishments were amazing, perhaps that is part of how they can have peace with less now. The rest of us may struggle not to shudder in self-awareness that what we did was the best that we will ever do.

Still, I think that personal peace and happiness are mostly choices. We can embrace what is possible and beautiful or despair with anger and resentment at what is gone and what we can't change.

I remember a scene from *Monty Python and the Holy Grail*, where a worker is pushing a cart of corpses through a plague-ridden bleak dark-age village, calling, "Bring out your dead!" A limp man is carried out and heaved onto the cart. He complains, "I'm not dead yet!" The three have a brief discussion before the cart pusher delivers the prone man a fatal club to the head.

"I'm not dead yet!" is the part I choose to focus on now.

Life is still here to enjoy. We can now engage in activities that would have been regarded as too tame in younger years yet are potentially just as inspiring. Age can enhance the love of others and nature and the sweetness of comradery. DVNP provides a reset for us from the frantic pace of modern life. Retirement from a regular job potentially allows for more time and scheduling flexibility. I must be missing part of the formula here because it is getting harder for us hikers to meet each year.

Here's an analogy that sometimes works for me. Previous volcanic flows that have had erosion eat at their perimeters form mesas, common in southwestern deserts. Mesas are high flat areas with steeply sloped sides. Life is a game metaphorically experienced on a vast, slightly sloped mesa, where in our youth we quickly play uphill to the gentle crest. As we age, the game becomes slower and inexorably shifts down the mesa's gradual grade towards the steep edge. I believe that my hiking buddies and I want to play as long as we can. If we haven't fallen off the edge we can still engage in the game.

The edges of mesas are very steep, and you generally can't climb back up if you fall off. My previous wife died at age forty-five, and in her last days she exuded a resigned peace—that this phase was ending, but it was still a really fine run. She left the mesa of her life more as a rising spirit than a falling body. I don't show any certain evidence of dying now, but I think I could accommodate it without deep regrets even if it came soon. I've had more and better years than many and have been privileged to a life in the richest place and time ever on this planet, often being loved more than I feel I deserved.

It is also a minor salve for me to know that in geologic terms, whatever humans do, it eventually won't matter much. In geologic and cosmic terms of time, it will all get erased and restructured by heavenly forces much greater than us. Still, it seems irresponsible and wicked to needlessly destroy and astoundingly pretentious for people to play God.

Several years ago in DVNP, the four of us discussed a movie called *The Bucket List*, wherein the characters played by Jack Nicholson and Morgan Freeman face their terminal cancers by doing everything daring and impractical that they wouldn't have considered previously. I think it was Johnny who suggested that our buckets are already full. He said that we'll just get bigger experiential buckets as we add more life and adventures. What a beautiful, positive concept.

Although many things have changed, I hope that our annual trips to DVNP can eventually resume. Due to COVID-19 still being virulent, 2021 doesn't look promising that way. Not knowing what is coming, it seems that now is a good time to share the stories. Besides, sometimes reading about adventures makes it easier to tolerate being stuck in the house.

This book tries to articulate how the annual DVNP adventures and their substitutes have shaped my psyche and hopefully taught me things of value. So, I'll wrap by saying that I believe we all should make the best of our adventures, however they are defined. Let's please also preserve and protect our planet in the loving interest of everything living, including the generations of people after us.

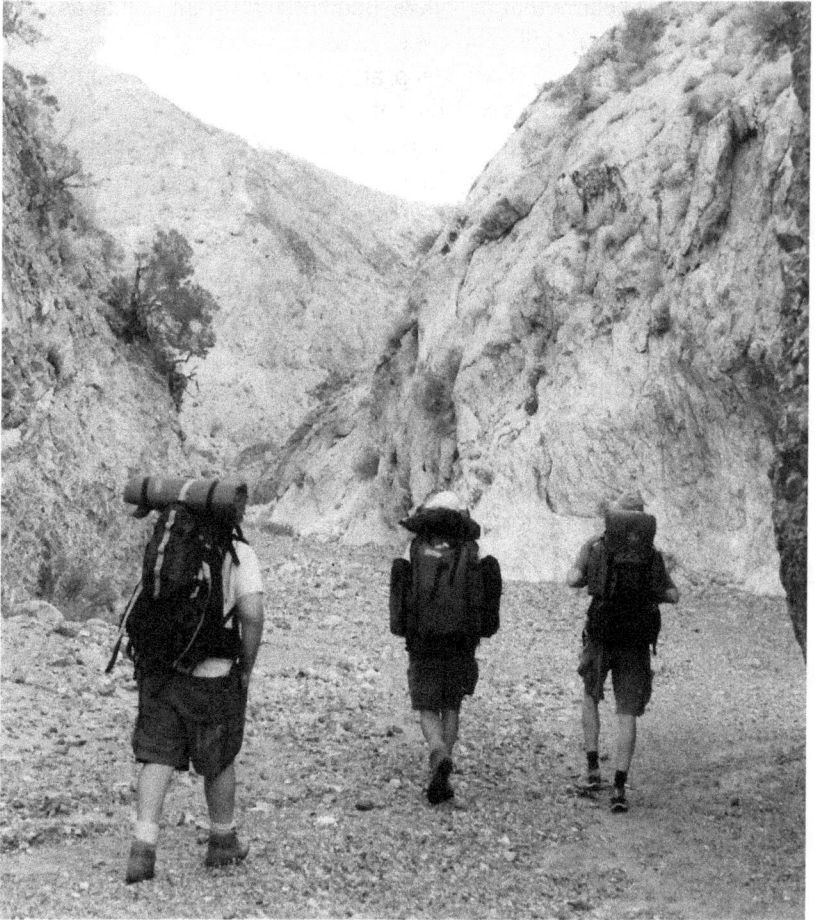

# Sources

Special thanks go to Michel Digonnet for sharing his hard-earned experiences and research with the rest of the world and inspiring us four hikers to have outdoor experiences in his wake.

Appreciation goes to John Soennichsen, who must be something of a kindred soul because he also subjected himself and some friends to unnecessarily life-threatening escapades.

Apologies go to the authors of the many articles, pamphlets, maps, and books about Death Valley that I have read, appreciated, and misplaced in the years since beginning these themed adventures.

Finally, much gratitude is offered to the numerous authors of books both academic and recreational on hiking, geology, and environmental themes that did not directly reference Death Valley but fueled my interest in that special place.

*The following publications were referenced in the book:*

Digonnet, Michel. *Hiking Death Valley: A Guide to Its Natural Wonders and Mining Past.* Palo Alto: Wilderness Press, 1999.

Reader's Digest. *The Most Scenic Drives in America.* Pleasantville, NY: The Reader's Digest Association, 1997.

Soennichsen, John. *Live from Death Valley: Dispatches from America's Low Point.* Seattle: Mountaineers Books, 2005.

# Acknowledgements

Thanks to John McDougal, Johnny Hagman, and Brad Lawson, who also share credit for these adventures. Voni Rock knowingly married this author and has demonstrated many years of tolerance for his behavior. My appreciation goes to Mary McLaughlin, who made the book intelligible, and Cathy Klein, who made it handsome enough to beguile you into purchasing it. Thanks also to you for sharing an appreciation for this special place in our wonderful world.

# About the Author

Ken Rock's first shared writing was at age six, when he used a crayon to print a younger brother's name behind the curtain on the living room wall. Although somewhat discouraged when his crayons were taken, he recovered enough as an adult to take on the job of writing operations and maintenance manuals for water and wastewater treatment facilities. That excitement was somehow not enough, so he also wrote a couple of film screenplays that Hollywood was not ready for.

His next paid writings were numerous technical memos outlining ways to save money in water operations. With this he had some success, perhaps because the subjects were too boring for others to finish reading and argue about. He then took on the editing of textbooks about water and wastewater treatment, finding that work less time consuming than writing on those subjects, yet somehow still not completely fulfilling.

Ken hopes that more creative writing such as *Hiking and Life Lessons: Partial Enlightenment from Death Valley* will keep the right side of his brain from withering too quickly. He has additional projects in mind as well.

His mother still has not returned his crayons.

www.ingramcontent.com/pod-product-compliance
Lightning Source LLC
Chambersburg PA
CBHW050124280326
41933CB00010B/1240